Cognitive Information Systems in Management Sciences

Cognitive Information Systems in Management Sciences

Lidia Ogiela
AGH University of Science and Technology,
Cryptography and Cognitive Informatics Research Group,
Krakow, Poland

Series Editor
Fatos Xhafa

ACADEMIC PRESS

An imprint of Elsevier
elsevier.com

Academic Press is an imprint of Elsevier
125 London Wall, London EC2Y 5AS, United Kingdom
525 B Street, Suite 1800, San Diego, CA 92101-4495, United States
50 Hampshire Street, 5th Floor, Cambridge, MA 02139, United States
The Boulevard, Langford Lane, Kidlington, Oxford OX5 1GB, United Kingdom

Notices
Knowledge and best practice in this field are constantly changing. As new research and experience broaden our
understanding, changes in research methods, professional practices, or medical treatment may become necessary.

Practitioners and researchers must always rely on their own experience and knowledge in evaluating and using
any information, methods, compounds, or experiments described herein. In using such information or methods
they should be mindful of their own safety and the safety of others, including parties for whom they have a
professional responsibility.

To the fullest extent of the law, neither the Publisher nor the authors, contributors, or editors, assume any liability
for any injury and/or damage to persons or property as a matter of products liability, negligence or otherwise, or
from any use or operation of any methods, products, instructions, or ideas contained in the material herein.

British Library Cataloguing-in-Publication Data
A catalogue record for this book is available from the British Library

Library of Congress Cataloging-in-Publication Data
A catalog record for this book is available from the Library of Congress

ISBN: 978-0-12-803803-1

For Information on all Academic Press publications
visit our website at https://www.elsevier.com/books-and-journals

Working together
to grow libraries in
developing countries

www.elsevier.com • www.bookaid.org

Publisher: Jonathan Simpson
Acquisition Editor: Sonnini R Yura
Editorial Project Manager: Ana Claudia Garcia
Production Project Manager: Kiruthika Govindaraju
Designer: Victoria Pearson

Typeset by MPS Limited, Chennai, India

I dedicate this book to my dearest mother Izydora,
to the memory of my dearest father Julian and brother Mariuszek
as well as to Ula, Marek and Waldemar,
whom I want to thank for all their support and help.

Contents

Biography

Computer scientist, mathematician, economist. She received Master of Science in mathematics from the Pedagogical University in Krakow, Poland, and Master of Business Administration in management sciences and marketing from AGH University of Science and Technology in Krakow, Poland, both in 2000. In 2005 she was awarded the title of Doctor of Computer Science and Engineering at the Faculty of Electrical, Automatic Control, Computer Science and Electronic Engineering of the AGH University of Science and Technology, for thesis and research on cognitive informatics and its application in intelligent information systems. In 2016 she received Habilitation degree in Computer Science from the Faculty of Electrical Engineering and Computer Science at VŠB—Technical University of Ostrava in Czech Republic. She is an

Prof. Dr. Lidia Ogiela

author of more than 150 scientific international publications on computer science, information systems, cognitive analysis techniques, cognitive economy and cognitive management, cryptography, and computational intelligence methods. She is a member of few prestigious international scientific societies as: SIAM—Society for Industrial and Applied Mathematics, as well as SPIE—The International Society for Optical Engineering, and CSS—Cognitive Science Society. Currently, she is at the associate professor position, and works at the AGH University of Science and Technology.

Foreword by Prof. Dr. Fang-Yie Leu

This book addresses a very important area of cognitive information systems, as the intersection of intelligent systems, management science, and cognitive informatics. For the readers, it is a novel book combining two main topics—intelligent cognitive information systems and management applications. The organization of this book is very systematic and professional. Author gradually introduces the reader to the concept of cognitive information systems, describing its origins, development until the presentation of examples of cognitive systems. Also the book, providing very good illustrations, can easily understand the described aspects. I would strongly recommend this book and encourage you to enjoy reading it.

Prof. Dr. Fang-Yie Leu
Database Systems and Network Security Laboratory
Chairperson of Big-data Master Program
Tunghai University, Taichung City, Taiwan

Foreword by Prof. Ing. Francesco Palmieri, Ph.D.

This book will be helpful in solving several key problems associated to managing huge amounts of data by using cognitive information systems and advanced management techniques. Therefore the author described very systematically the main topic of this book. First, she addressed the fundamentals of cognitive science and cognitive informatics. Second, the author also described the fundamentals of management sciences. Finally, we can read about the connections between intelligent cognitive information systems and management applications. Since, this proposition, presenting new aspects of semantic data interpretation, is a quite novel one, this book assumes significance in computer science technologies. This is also a very practical book, dedicated to all readers which would like to immediately understand cognitive solutions. I recommend this work and I believe that it will be a good reference for exploring knowledge about cognitive information systems.

Prof. Ing. Francesco Palmieri, Ph.D.
Department of Computer Science
University of Salerno, Salerno, Italy

Preface

Informatics is now developing very quickly and in various aspects. No one direction of development that dominates over others can be identified now, nor can areas be found in which such development is hard to see. Informatics offers a great treasure trove of various innovative solutions which drive not only the theoretical development of this discipline, but also practical solutions in areas in which no significant solutions were seen just a few years ago. This can be illustrated by the constantly improved topic of the artificial mind or the increasing miniaturization of cognitive robots. These are only selected directions in the development of information system theories and applications, but there are many more, and this is why it is worth going for new solutions commensurate to the times in which we live.

Systems for the semantic description interpretation of data are another innovative solution in the area of informatics. This group of solutions includes cognitive information systems which, after many years of development, have finally been formally described and presented.

This book is the product of research carried out by the author for many years. It was created as the result of work on the semantic analysis and interpretation of various datasets, which form the starting point for defining cognitive information systems. The purpose of the analytical approach presented in this book is to show that for in-depth analysis of data, the layers of semantics contained in these sets must be taken into account. Semantic analysis processes are used to describe and interpret data and make it possible to reason using the semantic information contained in the analyzed datasets. Such a perspective on analysis processes significantly supplements the capabilities of traditional analysis and means that the decision-making processes carried out are the result of the correct data analysis process.

Cognitive information systems are used in various areas of science and everyday life, but the main domain in which they will be demonstrated, used and described in this book are management processes (cognitive management).

I hope that the book I am presenting to you will allow important topics of cognitive science transferred to the realm of computer solutions to be presented in an interesting and exciting way to every reader. I also have great hopes that while reading this book, you, Dear Reader, will wonder whether the world around you is offering new, unexplored topics and whether it would be worthwhile to explore the secrets of knowledge that could be used to discover even more of the world's secrets.

Lidia Ogiela

Acknowledgment

Lidia Ogiela

AGH University of Science and Technology,
Cryptography and Cognitive Informatics Research Group,
Krakow, Poland

INTRODUCTION

The development of cognitive science within an area shared with computer science is becoming an important direction of the development of computer, technical, economic, and social sciences. It is also perceived as having a priority importance for the enhancement of research by scientific communities representing various areas of science. At the same time, it acts as an indicator for assessing the development of scientific disciplines and the level of innovation of units carrying out this type of research work. Both in the areas of science and of everyday life, and also at the interface of these two areas, it is clearly visible how cognitive science influences the progress in everyday life and becomes its determining factor. In addition, the level of development of economic, scientific, and state organizations is increasingly frequency benefiting from the cognitive aspects of interpreting and analyzing the reasons for the occurrence of various phenomena, assessing the degree of their progress and determining its directions. In addition, it is oriented toward the semantic assessment of the consequences of taking specific decisions as part of solving different problems.

This is the same perspective from which one should currently view the progress of computer science, which is now driving the rapid, strong development of information/cognitive science. This development makes it possible to assess problems, which form the foundations of information/cognitive science, like the tasks of analyzing and interpreting various datasets. This assessment is made possible by techniques of semantic perception, description, and characterization of the above datasets. So what makes it necessary to carry out this type of interpretation aimed at in-depth data analysis? In answer to this question one cannot but notice the very frequent reports we hear, but which we mostly treat as some novelties or curios from the technical realm. These novelties, frequently enhanced with elements of semantic and cognitive interpretation and features characteristic for the human mind, work on the interface between the real and virtual worlds. These worlds, their elements and characteristic features are increasingly frequently intertwined in our observations, knowledge, and often also everyday life. Thus one cannot help but try to understand what forms the basis of this type of activity and how far the virtual world can step in and influence our actions and decisions. This is the domain in which we should view the growth of computer and cognitive science that are now enjoying their heyday. Today also marks the renaissance of cognitive science, with regards to exploring the function and operation of perception, interpretation, understanding, analysis, and reasoning processes, which are characteristic for all decision-making processes taking place in the human mind. These processes, combined with algorithms developed based on applications taken from computer science, mathematics, and technology, have led to the formation of a broad new scientific discipline called cognitive informatics. With

Cognitive Information Systems in Management Sciences. DOI: http://dx.doi.org/10.1016/B978-0-12-803803-1.00001-X

regard to cognitive informatics, various directions of its development and opportunities for its application can be considered. Cognitive informatics will constitute the leading subject of this book, which is also a kind of guide to the subjects of cognitive informatics, cognitive information systems, and methods of using them for various data interpretation and analysis jobs. A particularly important direction of the application of cognitive information systems will cover management theory and information management tasks.

The author of this book was motivated by the constant development of cognitive/decision-making science which the author has described in previous publications, i.e., Refs. [1–6], and the wish to show the reader that the processes of automatic, semantic analysis of data can be effectively transferred to the domain of management theory. This type of solutions is aimed at enhancing the widely known decision-making processes which sometimes lead to a significant risk of the wrong decision being taken because of analyzing the wrong and incomplete datasets. To prevent such situations, the tasks of interpreting broad sets of information and decision-making tasks should be extended by adding the stage of semantic data analysis. These processes will be described in subsequent chapters of this book, which will present in detail the methods of semantically analyzing data and their orientation toward supporting decision-taking in management theory.

This type of problems has not yet been elaborated by other authors but only by the author of this book and the team closely cooperating with her in this research. This is why the contents presented in this book constitute proprietary achievements and an innovation from the scientific point of view.

This book is the result of work on systems for the cognitive analysis and interpretation of various, extensive datasets. The purpose of the analytical approach presented in this publication will be to show that for an in-depth analysis of data, the layers of semantics contained in these sets must be taken into account. These examples make it possible to not only precisely describe specific sets, phenomena, information, etc., but also allow their in-depth analysis. This approach to this subject was made possible by work to combine the subjects of intelligent information systems and the cognitive aspects taken from the operation of human methods of data analysis. The interdisciplinary nature of the solutions proposed means that the subject of cognitive systems forming part of cognitive informatics becomes a new challenge for the research and application work carried out.

While satisfying the readers' expectations of the publication of a book of this type, I dearly hope that this book will serve as a guide to the difficult, frequently ambiguous, and convoluted tasks of the semantic analysis of extended datasets and well demonstrate in an easy to understand way out how these tasks could be executed, e.g., in management theory. The method of applying the scientific solutions produced represents one of the possible directions of operation of the described cognitive systems, and the foundations for such solutions should be seen in cognitive informatics itself.

The author of this book hopes that her book will accurately guide readers on an interesting journey through the intricacies of information and cognitive science. It can thus make us wonder (sometimes jocularly), when we look at the world around us, whether we have really got to know it, whether we understand it, and whether we will ever be able to accurately and unambiguously (avoiding contradictions) explain what happens around us.

To introduce the reader to the world of cognitive science, the journey should start with the beginnings of this discipline. The first mentions of cognitive matters can be found in the works of Aristotle [7], the author of two basic, fundamental methods of classification describing all varieties of cognitive science in different ways. The fundamental element of Aristotelian considerations was the notion of a category, and his in-depth work has led to distinguishing the accidental category and the category of substances. These categories were distinguished based on the identifiable differences between the subject of a sentence understood as the substance and the predicate, which is the accidental category. The category of substances included notions which described and presented something substantive. They thus became "a specific substance," the subject of a sentence, something tangible. Within the accidental categories, Aristotle distinguished nine basic notions, which included quantity, quality, relation, place, time, location, state, action, and affection.

Aristotle's considerations gave rise to a method currently referred to as "*top-down*," which defines a concept based on the type (*genus*) and the appearance of a single or several differences (*differentiae*) allowing new types of forms to be distinguished from other forms of the same genus. Aristotle introduced and expanded theses of this type in works of a logical character, incessantly criticizing the limitations of this approach. He did this in works of a biological nature, while proposing an approach today commonly known as *bottom-up*, which starts from a precise description, definition, and indication of a given unit, classifying sets of units as a species within a genus and grouping individual genera into groups. The top-down method was right for presenting and describing the results of Aristotle's considerations of this method. Conversely, he indicated the *bottom-up* method as the best for discovering research processes of an object, a notion or a definition.

Aristotle's works were recognized, among others, by the ancient philosopher and astrologist Porphyry, who proposed the commentary to Aristotelian categorization in the 3rd century of common era. This commentary contained the first instance of using a tree in the form of a diagram showing categories and references to syllogisms with Aristotelian laws and rules concerning reasons associated with genera and types of defined subgenera. The diagram thus contained the descriptions of the perfect genus, genera, lower levels, subgenera, closest level, species and individual. This completed diagram made it possible to observe how different genera transform into other tree structures, how subtypes, lower levels, etc. develop for the described elements of the tree.

In subsequent years and centuries cognitive science developed, although it was not referred to by this name. The development of cognitive topics and simple solutions, which we would refer to as "applied" today, formed the foundation for the continuous development of cognitive science. One of the solutions worth remembering were the works of Gottfried Wilhelm Leibniz—*Characteristica Universalis* [8]—which made it possible to present simple sentences using numbers. In hindsight, it can be indisputably stated that the result of the work by Leibniz was a proposal of a universal dictionary. This dictionary was capable of translating words, sentences, or syllogisms into numbers which could be the subject of reasoning based on arithmetic rules. To simplify the calculations necessary, Leibniz also proposed the first computing machine capable of multiplying and dividing. Leibniz's works can thus be seen as the beginnings of computational linguistics. This discipline of science traces its beginnings to the definitions and implementation of Leibniz's dictionary [8].

When characterizing computational linguistic methods we must remember that the solutions used (which take the form of computer systems) transform high level notions (complex notions) into lower level notions, i.e., into words. Such a system may have a constructive form which makes it possible to build complex notions by assembling simple ones. This solution is most often treated as optional and not obligatory.

The last centuries have seen continuous attempts to take action and develop a theory which would in the end lead to creating a cognitive system. This solution was to be aimed at proposing a cognitive system that would make it possible to describe the human process of acquiring knowledge, and at the same time science would be able to describe similar processes taking place in a computer system. Methods leading to formal notations, creating definitions, logical and fuzzy methods as well as prototyping were developed. All of them were aimed at defining words, notions, meanings, etc.

The development of cognitive science constantly aimed at unambiguously identifying the basis of conditions responsible for the processes of learning and analyzing various states and situations. Cognitive science became one of the scientific disciplines answering the question about cognitive processes taking place in the human mind [9–11]. This is an experimental field of science researching various expressions of the cognitive activity of the mind. Human methods of analyzing information and states of mind accompanying these learning and understanding processes became a natural and extremely interesting subject of research, albeit hard to conceptualize theoretically and test empirically [12–14].

As part of work on the human cognitive process related to different scientific fields, the study of cognitive problems requiring the involvement of researchers from many different scientific disciplines started. An interest in expanding the scientific approach to studying the mind arose, to which the following contributed: researchers from computational disciplines, including:

- cybernetics—Norbert Wiener,
- information theory—John von Neumann,
- artificial intelligence—John McCarthy, Marvin Minsky, and Lotfi A. Zadeh,
- broad studies of the brain—Donald Olding Hebb, David Hubel, and Torsten Nils Wiesel,
- as well as theories of generative grammar in linguistics or of formal grammars—Noam Chomsky.

Cognitive science was seen as a science from the interface of different scientific disciplines from which it took its varied inspirations and on the foundations of which it started to grow (Fig. 1.1).

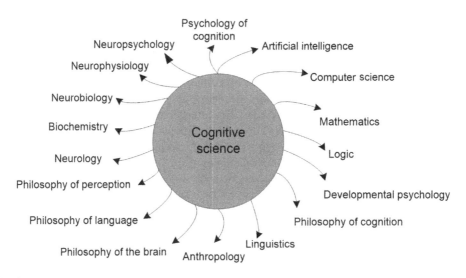

FIGURE 1.1

Disciplines making up cognitive science.

Scientific disciplines developing the field of cognitive science, at the same time aiming at machine-based solutions, were to demonstrate that the human mind can be presented in a system perspective, while processes of learning and understanding can be treated as a multistage computational process. From this perspective, every mental process taking place in the human mind is treated as information processing. The purpose of the computational view of cognitive processes is to create IT models of complex biological and psychological processes. In such matters the problem of the complexity of the object studied cannot be omitted. For this type of considerations, a model approach is extremely useful, because models can not only be created, but also experimentally studied using computer simulations, while the adequacy of these models is confronted with the neurobiological knowledge of the structures and functions of nervous system parts and elements, collected and constantly extended using new techniques of testing the brain biology.

One of the primary and at the same time most important reasons for the creation of cognitive science was understanding that the topic of learning turned out to be more complex than it was thought. To solve this problem, it was necessary to redistribute the research work between scientists dealing with the mind, psychology, and computer analyses. Thus cognitive science was distinguished by its multidisciplinary nature. The multidisciplinary nature of cognitive science was due to founding this science on many other disciplines which contributed to its development. The approach itself to subjects describing the operation of the human mind and the ability of transferring the results of this work to system (computer) solutions offered huge opportunities to science and practice. There was a lot of hope that if this work were successful, it would become possible to create a solution with the features of the human mind: artificial intelligence [15,16].

During research work it was observed that today's science can distinguish and research only small fragments of the complex set of problems associated with learning and understanding. Research covered selected cognitive problems, such as perception, imagination, memory, learning, abstract thinking, understanding, remembering, etc.

Cognitive science started being seen as a kind of synthesis of the knowledge about the mind enhanced with philosophical studies of its nature, the knowledge of psychological phenomena, and the rules governing the behavior of people and animals. The scope of this knowledge also had to include topics of research on language as well as the biological foundations of psychological phenomena, and even cybernetic topics. The scope of related basic research includes research on the brain and on the psychological aspects of its operation, the ways of describing them using mathematical models, and engineering methods of building a structure resembling the human brain to some extent, which could be used for development and improvement [17,18].

The basic areas which cognitive science deals with most frequently include the following [19–22]:

- impact of mega- and microinformation on human behavior,
- emotional modeling of human behavior,
- cultural modeling of human behavior,
- impact of the physical on the spiritual world,
- description of human impressions and their quality,
- consciousness function analysis,
- brain function interpretation,
- formal system design and determining the meaning of symbols,
- neural model design,

- technical aspects of artificial intelligence,
- mind–brain relationships.

Nowadays, cognitive topics are becoming the focus of various analyses carried out by different scientific disciplines. Today, cognitive science is understood as the science of learning and in this regard becomes inseparably connected with the theory of cognition, philosophy, psychology, medicine, linguistics, informatics, and also technology. Psychology plaid a special role in analyzing the states of the human mind when it performs analyses. Three basic perception phases have been distinguished in the processes of analyzing and understanding the information received and perceived by the human mind (Fig. 1.2) [21,23]:

- information recording—may boil down to a single act of perception, but may also take the form of a complex process,
- remembering—this perception phase may consist in the simple fixing in memory of detailed information, i.e., facts, patterns of objects, and methods of action, but in more complex situations may consist in creating a universal memory trace (a gnostic unit) during which features that are needed to understand new analyzed situations can be generated,
- coding of information obtained—in this perception phase, the information is hidden, encrypted, decrypted and divided, which is of particular importance in the process of information coding,
- storage—this is the latent stage of all mental processes that can occur,
- information retrieval—in this phase, remembering, recognizing, understanding, and relearning of specific new skills occur.

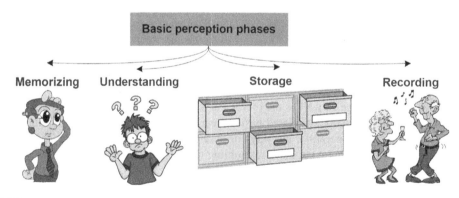

FIGURE 1.2

Basic perception phases.

From the point of view of cognitive science the most important phase is the retrieval phase which serves as a measure of human memory processes. This measure obviously refers to the processes of remembering, recognizing, understanding, and learning. Memory processes are inseparably linked to the occurrence of links between certain properties of the nervous system and individual analyzers in the human brain. The memory dependent on the analyzer type is called the peripheral ability. Another type of memory ability is the general ability, acting during the effect of complex stimuli, achieved as a result of the work of many analyzers. The most important features of memory used to assess the mental process include (Fig. 1.3):

- permanence—a criterion referring directly to the information storage stage,
- speed—defined as the ease of recording new, unknown facts and links between them, appears during the remembering phase,
- accuracy/fidelity—used to define the relationships between the retrieved information and the contents of the information acquired during the remembering phase,
- readiness—occurs during the retrieval phase, used to determine whether the recall process can be executed immediately, whether it runs without major difficulties or whether it is necessary for additional activating stimuli to occur, and
- range/capacity—relates to the coding phase.

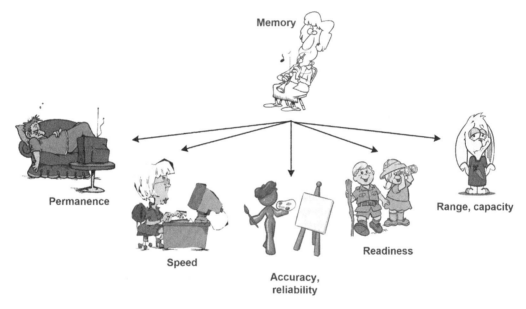

FIGURE 1.3

Memory features appearing during the information retrieval process.

From the perspective of cognitive science described in this book and oriented at semantic data analysis, the most important process our considerations will focus on is the recognition process. Recognition, as one of the memory stages, is linked with and implies the operation of perception and decision-making processes. These stages will be described in detail later.

Cognitive science subjects have been followed not only by social science, philosophy of psychology. They were developed with an equal interest also by technical science, particularly informatics and mathematics. One of the most important roles in cognitive analysis was played by artificial intelligence, which made it possible to create computer systems executing certain cognitive activities. In this regard, it has brought us closer to the execution of cognitive tasks by solutions designed by imitating the human mind. Its most important job became to develop application solutions that resembled the operation of the human mind as closely as possible. The success of the systems constructed was assessed by reference to their practical utility and the possibility of deploying them to conduct basic research on cognition. The topic of computer modeling appeared, which was also aimed at achieving a similarity of the artificial system to the human cognitive process. The development of cognitive topics by informatics meant that work started on tasks of computer understanding and reasoning, which, as a result, led to the development of computer cognitive science. This science also benefited a lot from the development of mathematics, from the scope of which it became possible to use the basics of analytical and semantic mathematics [24,25]. Mathematical structures used to analyze variable functions and operations were successfully used to build system architectures analyzing data in dynamic processes. A new scope of science at the interface of such scientific disciplines as cognitive informatics, computational intelligence, software engineering, knowledge engineering, and mathematics was defined. In recent years, Wang has called this field as denotational mathematics [26–28].

Doubtlessly, apart from the publications cited here so far, which describe the opportunities for using cognitive science to analyze various types of information, the application of cognitive topics to the computer analysis of data became a new idea for furthering cognitive science. This type of development, description, and design of cognitive structures leads to a structural and semantic analysis of various datasets. Structural analysis is based on applying cognitive methods to the information about the structure, the form and the shape of the analyzed object. On the other hand, semantic analysis uses the information contained within the datasets, i.e., the semantic information.

Nowadays, cognitive science topics are increasingly, frequently followed by other scientific disciplines with reference to which they had not originally been considered. The most important of those disciplines include economics, cryptography, logistics, automation, medicine, transport, and industry.

The incessant, accelerating development of cognitive science and also the ability to adapt it to various topics and analyses posits new, unsolved research problems to contemporary cognitive science. This is because we still do not know the answer to the question of the extent to which artificial solutions can imitate natural ones, the extent to which an artificial mind can follow the rules according to which the human cognitive process operates, whether it is possible to imitate the human thought process and the like.

However, we are certainly able to present solutions which are (possibly only to a small extent) designed by imitating the cognitive processes that can improve their operation. Such solutions designed as part of cognitive informatics and aimed at information management problems will form the subject of this book. For this purpose we will present cognitive analysis methods useful in the process of understanding economic standings and used to improve the operation and development of management support systems.

REFERENCES

[1] Ogiela L: Cognitive computational intelligence in medical pattern semantic understanding. In: *4th International Conference on Natural Computation ICNC'08, 18–20 October 2008, Jinan, China*, vol. 6, pp 245–247.
[2] Ogiela L: Computational intelligence in cognitive healthcare information systems. In: Bichindaritz I, Vaidya S, Jain A, Jain L, editors: *Computational intelligence in healthcare 4, advanced methodologies, studies in computational intelligence*, vol. 309, 2010, Springer-Verlag Berlin Heidelberg, pp 347–369.
[3] Ogiela L: Semantic analysis and biological modelling in selected classes of cognitive information systems. *Math Comput Model* 58(5–6):1405–1414, 2013.
[4] Ogiela L, Ogiela MR: *Cognitive techniques in visual data interpretation. Studies in computational intelligence* vol. 228, 2009, Springer-Verlag Berlin Heidelberg.

[5] Ogiela L, Ogiela MR: Semantic analysis processes in advanced pattern understanding systems. In Kim TH, Adeli H, Robles RJ, et al., editors: *Advanced computer science and information technology, communications in computer and information science, vol. 195, Conference: 3 rd international conference on Advanced Science and Technology (AST 2011), Jeju Island, South Korea, Jun 15–17, 2011*, pp 26–30.

[6] Ogiela L, Ogiela MR: *Advances in cognitive information systems*. Cognitive Systems Monographs COSMOS 17, 2012, Springer-Verlag Berlin Heidelberg.

[7] Aristotle McKeon R: The basic works of Aristotle, New York, NY, 1941, Random House Inc.

[8] Leibniz GW: *Dissertatio de arte combinatoria*, Leibnizens Mathematische Schriften 5, Georg Olms, Hildesheim, 1666.

[9] Albus JS, Meystel AM: Engineering of mind – an introduction to the science of intelligent systems, Hoboken, NJ, 2001, A Wiley-Interscience Publication John Wiley & Sons Inc.

[10] Anderson JR: The architecture of cognition, Cambridge, MA, 1983, Harvard Univ. Press.

[11] Atkinson RC, Shiffrin RM: Human memory, a proposed system and its control processes. In: Spence KW, Spence JT, editors: The psychology of learning and motivation: advances in research and theory, New York, NY, 1968, Academic Press, pp 89–195.

[12] Hubel D: Eye, brain and vision, New York, NY, 1988, W. H. Freeman.

[13] Kihlstrom JF: The cognitive unconscious. *Science* 237:1445–1452, 1987.

[14] Lazarus RS: Emotion and adaptation, New York, NY, 1991, Oxford University Press.

[15] Bender EA: Mathematical methods in artificial intelligence, Los Alamitos, CA, 1996, IEEE CS Press.

[16] Branquinho J, editor: The foundations of cognitive science, Oxford, 2001, Clarendon Press.

[17] Edelman S: Representation and recognition in vision, Cambridge, MA, 1999, MIT Press.

[18] Edwards W: *The theory of decision making* 51, 1953, Psychological Bulletin, pp. 380–417.

[19] Ogiela L: Cognitive systems for medical pattern understanding and diagnosis. In: Lovrek I, Howlett RJ, Jain LC, editors: Knowledge-based intelligent information and engineering systems, KES 2008, Part I, LNAI 5177, 2008, Springer-Verlag Berlin Heidelberg, pp 394–400.

[20] Ogiela L: *Modelling of cognitive processes for computer image interpretation*. In: Al-Dabass D, Nagar A, Tawfik H, Abraham A, Zobel R, editors: *EMS 2008 European Modelling Symposium, Second UKSIM European Symposium on Computer Modeling and Simulation, Liverpool, United Kingdom, 8–10 September 2008*, pp 209–213.

[21] Ogiela L: Cognitive informatics in automatic pattern understanding and cognitive information systems. In: Wang Y, Zhang D, Kinsner W, editors: *Advances in cognitive informatics and cognitive computing, studies in computational intelligence (SCI)*, vol. 323, 2010, Springer-Verlag Berlin Heidelberg, pp 209–226.

[22] Schachter S, Singer J: Cognitive, social and physiological determinants of emotional state. *Psychological Review* 63:379–399, 1962.

[23] Ogiela L: Pattern classifications in cognitive informatics. In: Ogiela M, Jain L, editors: *Computational intelligence paradigms in advanced pattern classification, studies in computational intelligence*, vol. 386, 2012, Springer-Verlag Berlin Heidelberg, pp 39–57.

[24] Ogiela L: Innovation approach to cognitive medical image interpretation. In: *Innovation'08, 5th international conference on innovations in information technology, Al Ain, United Arab Emirates, December 16–18, 2008*, pp 722–726.

[25] Ogiela L: UBIAS systems for the cognitive interpretation and analysis of medical images. *Opto-Electron Rev* 17(2):166–179, 2009.

[26] Wang Y: *On cognitive informatics, brain and mind. Transdisciplinary J Neurosci Neurophilos* 4(2):151–167, 2003.

[27] Wang Y: The theoretical framework of cognitive informatics. *Int J Cognit Informatics Nat Intell* 1(1):1–27, 2007.

[28] Wang Y: The cognitive processes of formal inferences. *Int J Cognit Informatics Nat Intell* 1(4):75–86, 2007.

THE FUNDAMENTALS OF COGNITIVE INFORMATICS

The fundamentals of cognitive informatics should be searched for in informatics dealing with the semantic interpretation and analysis of various datasets. The aspects of the semantic description and interpretation of information (data) aim this area of analysis at the semantic interpretation of data and the assessment of its meaning [1,2]. Tasks of describing and interpreting data based on cognitive subjects, which are at the same time an attempt to assess the meaning of the semantic content collected in these sets, have become the basis for formulating the claim that automatic interpretation of data is not limited to just the correct classification or recognition of analyzed data, but is primarily used to assess the impact of the meaning of the analyzed data on the broadest possible external situation. This situation can be the conditions prevailing outside the analyzed entity, like the competitive markets on which specific enterprises operate, but it can also be the situation that describes another, independently occurring condition, which can be assessed by reference to the analyzed state.

Thus the foundations of cognitive informatics should be looked for in research carried out at the interface of technology, informatics, neural science, and psychology. In this regard, it is possible to indicate common points from the interface of various scientific disciplines, at which different areas of knowledge that influence the development of cognitive science, decision-making theory, linguistics, and biology meet.

When talking about the origins of cognitive informatics, one cannot but mention research described in a report of 1978, which stated that cognitive science is an attempt to synthesize the problems researched as part of six basic, traditional scientific disciplines [3]:

- philosophy,
- psychology,
- linguistics,
- informatics,
- anthropology: philosophical, biological, and sociological,
- neural science.

The basis for defining cognitive science was provided by the observation that all the disciplines described earlier have certain common features, and it is thus possible to link them and find their common elements. These linkages indicated the presence of research areas shown in Fig. 2.1.

Cognitive Information Systems in Management Sciences. DOI: http://dx.doi.org/10.1016/B978-0-12-803803-1.00002-1

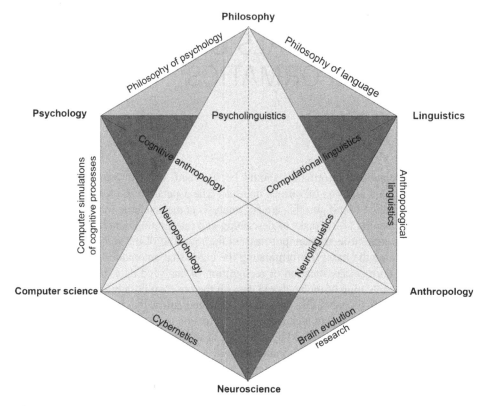

FIGURE 2.1

Sciences making up cognitive science and links between them.

Developed on the basis of Bechtel W, Abrahamsen A, Graham G: The live of cognitive science. In: Bechtel W, Graham G, editors:
A companion of cognitive science. Oxford, 1998, Blackwell Publishers, pp 1–104 [4]; Cohen H, Lefebvre C, editors: Handbook of
categorization in cognitive science. The Netherlands, 2005, Elsevier [5]; Ogiela L, Ogiela MR: Beginnings of cognitive science. In:
Ogiela L, Ogiela MR, editors: Advances in cognitive information systems, Cognitive Systems Monographs, COSMOS 17. Springer-
Verlag Berlin Heidelberg, 2012, pp 1–18 [6].

Based on the definition and identification of the main scientific disciplines making up cognitive science, it became possible to define the links between six main scientific disciplines within the area of which cognitive science was distinguished as a kind of bridge between them.

Thus cognitive science was understood as the bridge linking main scientific disciplines from among the many different ones. This bridge made it easier to understand how one scientific discipline influences another and what common elements link each of those disciplines to another. Hence not only were disciplines linking any two scientific sciences established, but the main direction of activity was to indicate the common part of all the basic areas of knowledge making up this analyzed state. The work carried out to determine the common parts made it possible to define cognitive science, science that had previously not been sufficiently identified or unambiguously defined it as it is constantly developing and incessantly borrowing from other sciences.

2.1 BASIC FORMALISMS OF COGNITIVE INFORMATICS

Cognitive informatics is understood as the combination of cognitive science topics and computer science. This combination is possible thanks to defining information mechanisms that may be used to describe and interpret processes taking place in the human mind. The basis for the operation of cognitive science is the ability to use human intelligence to combine its characteristic features with engineering applications. This new scientific discipline covers the use of mathematical theories and descriptions to describe and analyze data and information presented in the form of broad knowledge bases, as well as engineering disciplines including computer science, cognitive science, neuropsychology, systems theory, cybernetics, computer engineering, knowledge engineering, and computational engineering [7].

The foundations of cognitive informatics refer to mathematical notions, while formal models used to describe the theory of cognitive informatics come from the area of computational intelligence. Computational intelligence used to describe cognitive theories is derived from human and machine ways of analyzing information. Currently the most important applications of cognitive informatics concern the following areas:

- cognitive computers,
- cognitive knowledge bases,
- cognitive simulations of human mind operation,
- autonomous agent systems,
- cognitive robots,
- avatars and computational intelligence.

Cognitive informatics is now considered to be a science aiming to carry out interdisciplinary research in the areas of computer science, cybernetics, cognitive science, neuropsychology, knowledge engineering, computational intelligence, life science, and neural science. The combination of these varied scientific disciplines and an attempt to extract from them, aspects of analysis, understanding, and information processing has, in a sense, become a starting point to define the area of cognitive informatics [8–12]. And thus, firstly, all research problems from the cognitive informatics scope that are analyzed are aimed at understanding the operation of human intelligence mechanisms and cognitive processes running in the human mind. Secondly the understanding of the operation of cognitive mechanisms is transferred to the realm of engineering solutions to design computer solutions that can imitate (to a greater or lesser extent) the operation of the human mind. The basis for building this type of solutions is the presence of models of data perception and analysis as well as methods of acquiring knowledge necessary in analysis processes, and an attempt to describe them.

So what distinguishes cognitive informatics from other engineering solutions?

When answering this question one must note that even at the beginning of identifying this discipline of informatics as oriented at the cognitive, semantic analysis of information, this information was understood as an element distinguished from the reality surrounding us. This element (information) may be presented as a characteristic representative of the entire group of similar, semantically convergent information. The second case described information as a totally new element, a kind of exception, a component not previously known or analyzed, about which we have no knowledge.

This two-way view of information shows that the processes of information analysis and interpretation cannot be carried out schematically, in the same way in every information analysis process. It is therefore a process during which complex and ambiguous tasks are performed. This complexity and ambiguity results from the essence of the analysis process taking place in the human brain. On this basis, one can try to understand the essence of the entire reasoning process carried out using the information one has. The ability to correctly assess the situation and describe the analyzed information sets should lead to their correct analysis. In the work to unambiguously identify the notion of cognitive informatics it was necessary to formulate an unambiguous definition:

Cognitive informatics is understood as the combination of cognitive sciences and informatics intended to study the mechanisms by which information processes operate in the human mind, these processes being seen as elements of natural intelligence, and may be applied to engineering and technical tasks using an interdisciplinary approach [6,13].

The proposed definition of cognitive informatics allowed the unambiguous identification of areas in which its application will allow previous solutions to be supported, thus indicating the directions of its future development. The most important of them include the development of:

- IT systems aimed at the semantic analysis of data,
- cognitive robots and avatars,
- processes of analyzing human behaviors with a view to creating their automatic (artificial) counterparts.

The development of cognitive science, and in particular cognitive informatics, is seen in two categories [12]:

- the application view of informatics, computer technologies, and cognitive research tasks which include memory, learning, reasoning, concluding, and analysis,
- the use of cognitive theories to solve problems in computer science, knowledge engineering, software engineering, and computational intelligence.

These problems can be solved by applying the theoretical bases of processes running in the human brain, the most important of which include:

- the tasks of obtaining and acquiring information,
- the choice of information representation,
- the memory process,
- the recovery of lost information,
- generating information and knowledge,
- the communication process.

2.2 DATA ANALYSIS TECHNIQUES

The most important solution used to semantically analyze data is the process consisting in extracting semantic information contained in these sets. To make this process executable, it is necessary to relate it to processes running in the human mind, because that is where the most complete data analysis is executed. This is why, in semantic analysis, the most important role is played by processes modeled on the cognitive and decision-making processes occurring in human minds. Particular attention must be paid to the processes of describing, analyzing, and interpreting the meaning of information sets, i.e., meaning contained in the analyzed datasets. The processes cited are inseparably associated with the analysis of meaning, during which a special role is played by semantic analysis.

Semantic analysis forms the basis for the operation of cognitive information systems. When this semantic data analysis is conducted, several different processes occur: interpretation, description, analysis, and reasoning.

The main stages of semantic analysis are as follows:

- the stage of data preprocessing, which includes the processes of filtering and segmenting, the approximation stage and encoding,
- data representation, consisting of the definition of primitives, the process of defining relations between these primitives, and determining the relations between objects,
- linguistic perception,
- syntactic analysis,
- pattern classification,
- data classification,
- feedback,
- cognitive resonance,
- data understanding.

The majority of the semantic analysis stages presented apply to the process of data understanding. Starting with the syntactic analysis process executed using the formal grammar defined in the system, the stages during which we attempt to identify the analyzed data taking into consideration its semantics are executed sequentially. Data semantics is understood as the meaning contained in these datasets. The process of recognizing the analyzed datasets becomes the basis of further analysis stages, i.e., the cognitive analysis.

The traditional data analysis process is executed by defining the characteristic properties of these sets. As a result of this process a decision is taken which is the result of the data analysis process carried out (Fig. 2.2).

The classical process of data analysis is very frequently carried out in situations in which the analyzed sets are described in simple terms. In such a situation the expected information consists in only a simple characterization of data undergoing the analysis. However, such a way of analysis data is not always sufficient. This is because we frequently expect the analysis process to produce "some indication," a decision that would allow us to make the full use of the analyzed datasets. This is why the data analysis process can be enhanced with the cognitive analysis process. This second process consists in distinguishing consistent and inconsistent pair as a result of generating sets of features characteristic for the analyzed set. In addition, when this process is executed, expectations concerning the analyzed data are generated based on the expert knowledge base collected in the system. As a result of comparing feature-expectation pairs, cognitive resonance occurs, which is to identify consistent pairs and inconsistent pairs, significant in the ongoing analysis process. In cognitive analysis the consistent pairs are used to understand the meaning of the analyzed datasets (Fig. 2.3).

Due to the way it is carried out and the grammatical formalisms used, semantic analysis forms the foundation for the operation of cognitive information systems. Semantic analysis processes form the

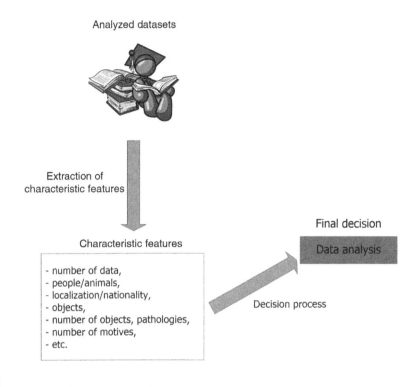

Analyzed datasets

Extraction of characteristic features

Final decision

Characteristic features

Data analysis

- number of data,
- people/animals,
- localization/nationality,
- objects,
- number of objects, pathologies,
- number of motives,
- etc.

Decision process

FIGURE 2.2

Components of the data analysis process.

cornerstone of the constantly developing, new scientific discipline—cognitive informatics. Cognitive informatics has thus become the starting point for a formal approach to interdisciplinary considerations of running semantic analyses in various cognitive areas. Semantics can be identified using a formal grammar defined in the system and a specified set of productions.

The productions defined make it possible to execute a linguistic reasoning algorithm. This is why the definition of algorithms of linguistic perception and reasoning forms the key stage in building a cognitive system. This process is based on a grammatical analysis aimed at examining semantic consistency. This is because it is necessary to answer the question whether the analyzed dataset is semantically correct (by reference to the defined grammar) or not.

In the first case, if the consistency is confirmed, the system carries out the analysis, as a result of which the consistency is determined and the appropriate name is assigned. If the consistency cannot be proven, the system stops the analysis. The lack of semantic consistency may be due to various reasons. The most frequent reasons for the lack of semantic consistency include [14]:

- the wrong definition of the formal grammar,
- no definition of the appropriate semantic reference,

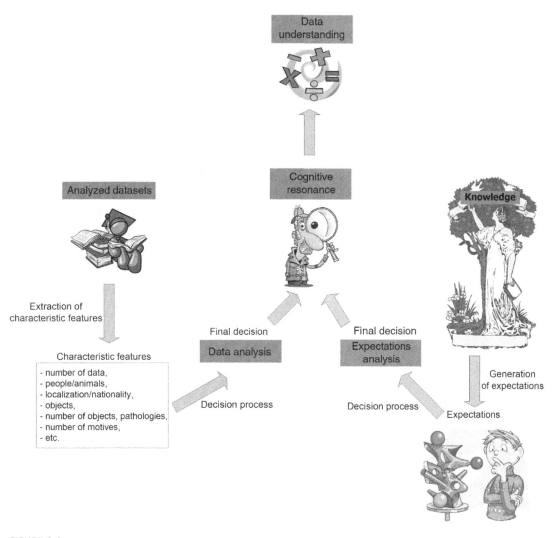

FIGURE 2.3

Semantic analysis and the data understanding processes.

- the insufficient or wrong definition of the pattern,
- a representative from outside the recognizable data class accepted for analyzing.

The cases described earlier lacking semantic consistency are the reasons for failing to find semantic consistency between the analyzed individual and the formal language defined in the analysis process. If a situation occurs in which semantic consistency is not determined, the definition process must be rerun, as an error may have crept in at any stage of it.

The semantic analysis executed in cognitive systems uses a linguistic approach for its operation. This approach is built on the basis of and by imitating the cognitive and decision-making processes running in the human brain. These are used for the semantic analysis of various datasets. In the systemic approach, just as in the human mind, the course of these processes is determined based on the way the human cognitive system works. This system thus becomes the foundation for designing cognitive data analysis systems.

The characteristic feature of cognitive systems is that data analysis occurs in three stages. This split is presented in Fig. 2.4.

Fig. 2.4 shows three independent stages of data analysis. The first one is the traditional data analysis, which includes qualitative and quantitative analysis processes. The results obtained at this stage are enhanced with the linguistic presentation of the analyzed dataset. The ability to linguistically describe data forms the basis for extracting semantic features from datasets. Determining the meaning of the data forms the basis of the second analysis stage, i.e., the semantic analysis. The semantic analysis is carried out by identifying the linguistic data perception and analysis using grammar formalisms. This makes it possible to execute the data analysis process, referred to as the cognitive data analysis. The completion of the cognitive data analysis leads to interpreting the results produced, based on the previously obtained semantic data notations. The assessment of the results produced represents the process of data understanding and reasoning on its basis to project the changes that may occur in the future.

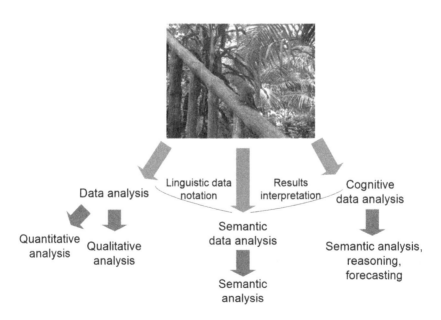

FIGURE 2.4

Stages distinguished in the operation of cognitive systems.

2.3 **COGNITIVE RESONANCE COMPUTER MODEL FOR DATA ANALYSIS**

A cognitive information system executes data analysis processes that can be carried out using the characteristic features of the analyzed datasets. This system has knowledge, in the form of knowledge bases, which becomes the basis for generating system expectations during the entire analysis process. These expectations are generated automatically using the expert knowledge bases held in the system. This system carries out an analysis aimed at determining characteristic features and indicating this type of features for the analyzed datasets. As a result of combining significant features characteristic for the analyzed datasets with the expectations generated by the system using the knowledge it holds and determining the consistency between them, cognitive resonance occurs (Fig. 2.5) [15,16]. If there is no consistency between the generated expectations and the expert knowledge, a dissonance occurs. This second phenomenon means that the semantic analysis process has failed. It is therefore of no interest from the scientific point of view, as it does not solve any scientific or practical problem, and consequently it will be omitted from our further considerations.

In the cognitive analysis process, expectation generation relates to the semantic contents of the analyzed datasets. Thus cognitive resonance forms the starting point in the entire process of understanding the analyzed information sets. This phenomenon progresses as described later. The stream of expectations produced by generating knowledge concerning the analyzed data and which can be derived using the semantic information contained in the datasets is compared to the elements of knowledge resources to determine similarities (consistencies). Knowledge resources are collected in the system in the form of expert knowledge bases. A comparison of the expectations with the knowledge distinguishes pairs of consistent expectations and characteristic features. If these pairs are consistent, they can gain importance (become significant), or conversely, they become insignificant. This process, by causing cognitive resonance, leads to confirming one of the possible hypotheses (in the case of data whose content can be understood), or conversely shows an inconsistency of expectations with characteristic features. This

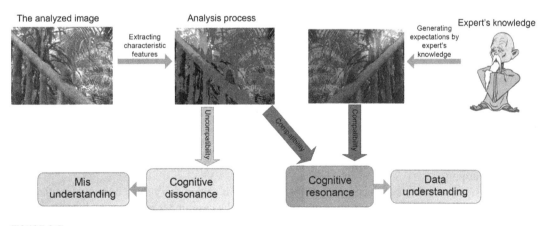

FIGURE 2.5

Cognitive resonance process.

situation is equivalent to the inconsistency of features and expectations that cannot be eliminated. The first case represents a success of the cognitive data analysis and the second case represents a failure of the semantic data interpretation [1,17].

Semantic data analysis systems use structural reasoning techniques for the correct matching of patterns [18,19]. The structure of the pattern depends on the type of data analyzed. The most characteristic structure is that of an image, as it has a complex form, usually containing multiple objects. In this case, the structure of the image is compared to the structure of the data constituting the image pattern. This comparison is made possible by introducing strings of derivative rules which allow a pattern to be unambiguously generated. Derivative rules are called productions and are defined in the grammar that defines the formal language. The recognized data is assigned to the class to which the pattern representing it belongs.

The cognitive analysis processes also refer to the syntactic approach, which makes use of functional blocks in the process of semantic analysis and interpretation. In the analysis process, the input image undergoes preprocessing during which the following stages are executed:

- filtering and preprocessing of the input image,
- approximating the shapes or locations of the analyzed objects,
- coding the image with terminal elements of the introduced description language.

After these stages are completed, the image has been represented anew in the form of hierarchical structures of a semantic tree and subsequent steps of deriving this representation from the initial symbol of the grammar.

During data preprocessing, cognitive information systems which carry out data identification analysis segment this data, identify primitives, and determine the relations between them. The classification proper consists in recognizing whether the given representation of input data belongs to the class of data generated by the formal language defined by one of the grammars that can be introduced. The grammars that can be defined are sequential, tree, or graph. Identification analysis processes are carried out using syntactic analysis [20,21].

2.4 EXTENDED COGNITIVE RESONANCE LEARNING ABILITIES FOR DECISION PROCESSES

Traditional semantic analysis systems are used to assess, analyze, and interpret data using the knowledge collected in the system (which is in a sense closed). It is therefore important to ask how the system will behave if, during the analysis process, data appears about which it has no knowledge and which it cannot classify to any counterpart (a similar element) it knows. In this case it is necessary to modify the proposed solutions to such extent that the system can learn new solutions. Because of this aspect, the processes of semantic data analysis were enhanced with new system operation stages, i.e., stages of system learning.

If the system encounters an incomprehensible situation, it cannot carry out a correct classification and pattern matching and it will not be able to understand the case under analysis. A situation that is incomprehensible to the system can, e.g., be one so far not defined in its knowledge base. If such a condition occurs, the system is expected to attempt to recognize the data by supplementing the knowledge base with new cases of pattern classification and data understanding. This supplementation is possible by adding new, previously undefined cases to the knowledge base.

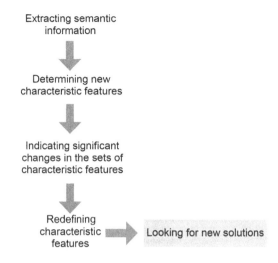

FIGURE 2.6

The process of teaching new solutions to a system.

The process by which the system learns is presented in Fig. 2.6.

The process of teaching new solutions to a system consists of five phases:

- extracting additional semantic information of significance in the subsequent analysis process,
- determining new (additional) characteristic features for the solution obtained before the system training process—extracting additional features may lead to changing the solution produced at the first stage, e.g., as a result of defining new patterns,
- indicating significant changes in the area of characteristic features, leading to optimizing the best solution established,
- redefining characteristic features,
- looking for new solutions based on the set of characteristic features and the expert knowledge base to which new elements of knowledge have been added.

The ability to enhance data analysis processes by adding new stages of semantic analysis that can be carried out because the system has been taught new solutions means that cognitive resonance is repeated many times in the data analysis process. If there are subsequent repetitions, it is possible to multiply the teaching process with the aim of the correct and complete data analysis. Enhancing the processes of semantic data analysis by teaching new solutions to the system means that the analysis processes are more extensive and can carry out the full semantic interpretation of information (Fig. 2.7).

In the process of teaching new solutions to cognitive systems, the entire analysis process is repeated based on the cognitive resonance. Unlike in the initial analysis process, this is based on extended sets of analyzed data and an extended base of expert knowledge. Both the new, extended set of the analyzed data and the expert knowledge base enhanced with new elements become the main foundation of cognitive data analysis processes in the proposed, new cognitive systems.

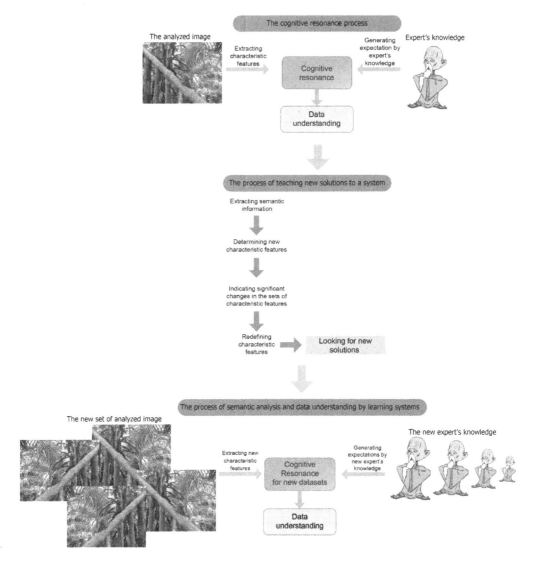

FIGURE 2.7

The process of semantic analysis and data understanding by learning systems.

REFERENCES

[1] Ogiela L: Syntactic approach to cognitive interpretation of medical patterns. In: Xiong C, Liu H, Huang Y, Xionh Y, editors: Intelligent robotics and applications, First international conference, ICIRA 2008, Wuhan, China, 15–17 October 2008, LNAI 5314, Springer-Verlag Berlin Heidelberg, 2008, pp 456–462.
[2] Ogiela L: Semantic analysis in cognitive UBIAS & E-UBIAS systems. *Comput Math Appl* 63(2):378–390, 2012.

[3] Wang Y, Zhang D, Latombe JC, Kinsner W, editors: *Proc. 7th IEEE International Conference on Cognitive Informatics (ICCI'08), IEEE CS Press, Stanford University, CA, USA, July, 2008*.

[4] Bechtel W, Abrahamsen A, Graham G: The live of cognitive science. In: Bechtel W, Graham G, editors: A companion of cognitive science, Oxford, 1998, Blackwell Publishers, pp 1–104.

[5] Cohen H, Lefebvre C, editors: Handbook of categorization in cognitive science, The Netherlands, 2005, Elsevier.

[6] Ogiela L, Ogiela MR: Beginnings of cognitive science. In: Ogiela L, Ogiela MR, editors: Advances in cognitive information systems, Cognitive Systems Monographs, COSMOS 17, 2012, Springer-Verlag Berlin Heidelberg, pp 1–18.

[7] Ogiela MR, Ogiela L: Cognitive informatics in medical image semantic content understanding. In: Kim TH, Stoica A, Chang RS, editors: *Security-enriched urban computing and smart grid, communication in computer and information science, vol. 78, 1st international conference on security-enriched urban computing and smart grid, Daejeon, South Korea, September 15–17, 2010*, pp 131–138.

[8] Davis LS, editor: Foundations of image understanding, Norwell, MA, 2001, Kluwer Academic Publishers.

[9] Edelman S: Representation and recognition in vision, Cambridge, MA, 1999, MIT Press.

[10] Gabrieli JDE: Cognitive neuroscience of human memory. *Annu Rev Psychol* 49:87–115, 1998.

[11] Ogiela L: Cognitive informatics in automatic pattern understanding and cognitive information systems. In: Wang Y, Zhang D, Kinsner W, editors: *Advances in cognitive informatics and cognitive computing, Studies in Computational Intelligence (SCI)*, vol. 323, 2010, Springer-Verlag Berlin Heidelberg, pp 209–226.

[12] Ogiela MR, Ogiela L: Towards new classes of intelligent cognitive information systems for semantic pattern classification. *Comput Informatics* 30(6):1099–1114, 2011.

[13] Wang Y: *On cognitive informatics, brain and mind. Transdisciplinary J Neurosci Neurophilos* 4(2):151–167, 2003.

[14] Ogiela L: Cognitive computational intelligence in medical pattern semantic understanding. In: *4th International Conference on Natural Computation ICNC'08, 18–20 October 2008, Jinan, China*, vol. 6, pp 245–247.

[15] Ogiela L: Cognitive systems for medical pattern understanding and diagnosis. In: Lovrek I, Howlett RJ, Jain LC, editors: Knowledge-based intelligent information and engineering systems, KES 2008, Part I, LNAI 5177, 2008, Springer-Verlag Berlin Heidelberg, pp 394–400.

[16] Ogiela L: UBIAS systems for the cognitive interpretation and analysis of image data. *Przegląd Elektrotechniczny* 84(5):14–23, 2008.

[17] Ogiela L: *Modelling of cognitive processes for computer image interpretation*. In: Al-Dabass D, Nagar A, Tawfik H, Abraham A, Zobel R, editors: *EMS 2008 European modelling symposium, Second UKSIM European symposium on computer modeling and simulation, Liverpool, United Kingdom, 8–10 September 2008*, pp 209–213.

[18] Ogiela L: Innovation approach to cognitive medical image interpretation. In: *Innovation'08, 5th international conference on innovations in information technology, Al Ain, United Arab Emirates, December 16–18, 2008*, pp 722–726.

[19] Ogiela L: Computational intelligence in cognitive healthcare information systems. In: Bichindaritz I, Vaidya S, Jain A, Jain L, editors: *Computational intelligence in healthcare 4, advanced methodologies, studies in computational intelligence*, vol. 309, 2010, Springer-Verlag Berlin Heidelberg, pp 347–369.

[20] Duda RO, Hart PE, Stork DG: Pattern classification, ed 2, New York, NY, 2001, A Wiley-Interscience Publication John Wiley & Sons, Inc.

[21] Minsky M: Semantic information processing, Cambridge, MA, 1968, MIT Press.

INTELLIGENT COMPUTER DATA ANALYSIS TECHNIQUES

3

Nowadays the progress in information techniques and technologies is accelerating, strengthening, and striking out in various directions, hence increasing their importance. This progress means that these techniques are becoming more and more significant not only from the theoretical standpoint, but mainly because of the practical perception of the ability to use different solutions in various spheres of life. This fact is confirmed by the fast growth of the Internet, fields that make use of computer and ICT networks, nanotechnology, military and defense technologies, logistics as well as knowledge and information management strategies. Virtual trade, electronic business, and electronic banking can illustrate such applications. The development of the technologies cited earlier means that all results obtained are used in various knowledge disciplines, and then adopted in practical solutions. A special case of such applications is the design of intelligent information systems dedicated to various uses, such as medicine, defense, cryptography, or management [1–4].

The analysis of information systems is certainly very complex, while their synthesis can be ambiguous because the type of action that has to be taken when designing a new information system depends on the type of this system as well as of the one at our disposal. Currently the following types of information systems are distinguished [5,6]:

- management information systems,
- data/information/knowledge management systems,
- expert systems,
- quality assurance systems,
- GIS systems,
- spatial information systems,
- decision-support systems,
- real-time systems,
- semantic data interpretation and analysis systems,
- personal identification systems.

Information system classification is not exhaustive as new classes of systems that are created constantly add various directions of use and analysis capabilities to this classification. However, it should be kept in mind that knowing the current classification helps correctly select the methods and techniques for further developing information systems.

Because of the broad opportunities for using the information systems designed, it is extremely important to point out the areas and disciplines to which they are dedicated. This makes it much simpler then to identify the ways and methods of solving problems which will be handled by the designed information systems. This is undoubtedly a very important aspect in the design of information systems because of the broadening list of disciplines in which information systems are used, and they are becoming important, indispensable tools. The primary disciplines in which information systems are used are presented in Fig. 3.1.

Every discipline presented in Fig. 3.1, in which information systems are applied, uses various types of systems as well as various methods of designing and implementing solutions with regard to the design of information systems of the appropriate type. The group of management information systems includes [7]:

- traditional systems with basic functionalities used to manage information and knowledge, and
- intelligent information systems created for the advanced support of decision-making processes.

Intelligent information systems have special characteristics, because they are envisaged for the in-depth analysis of the data which the system has access to and which it uses to carry the analysis out. From this perspective, intelligent information systems are thus:

- dedicated to disciplines identified at the definition stage,
- varied in terms of design and structure, depending on the type of system,
- varied in how they operate,
- varied in the ways of obtaining information and knowledge,
- varied in terms of:
  - collecting and storing information,
  - the type of data analyzed,
  - the method of transferring and processing information,

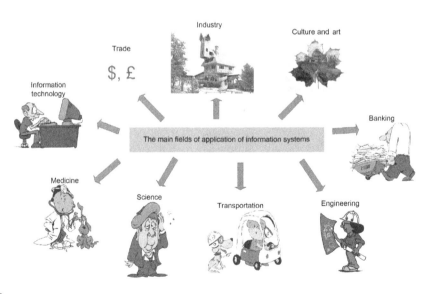

FIGURE 3.1

Disciplines where information systems are applied.

- the methods of interpreting, analyzing, recognizing, and understanding the datasets described and analyzed.

Intelligent information systems are characterized according to various description concepts. Among those used most often, there are IT tools for defining such types of systems, while modern solutions are designed using mathematical, logical, and philosophical methods of describing information systems. Every one of those concepts employs different theoretical formalism designed for drawing up the above system description (Fig. 3.2).

In order to correctly and comprehensively analyze an information system, all the above description concepts should be taken into account. In the case of intelligent information systems, mathematical concepts are used for the semantic analysis of data. These concepts are utilized to describe and semantically interpret data, and in particular to understand this data. The most useful formalism is the mathematical concept of the information system description [8–11]. However, it should be stressed that the remaining two concepts can also be used to describe intelligent information systems, and their additional advantage is that they are clearer than the aforementioned mathematical concept. So what distinguishes these concepts? Mainly the algorithms are used for the description activities and the complexity of the proposed solutions. The complexity of mathematical formalisms allows much better results to be produced than the remaining methods.

Mathematical formalisms are more accurate and unambiguous. To establish the correct way of operating information systems, methods of creating intelligent information systems and techniques of their description must be taken into account. The literature of the subject mentions three types of methods of creating and specifying information systems. These are as follows:

- structural,
- incremental, and
- object-based.

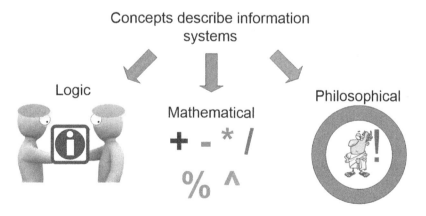

FIGURE 3.2

Information system description concepts.

Today is the heyday of structural methods because they can be used for diverse tasks of the semantic interpretation of data and information [12–14]. This development direction of structural analysis is in line with the topic undertaken in this book. This is because the development of intelligent information systems is based on the use of syntactic methods for data description and analysis. This process is then used to analyze set of data and information, and to understand their meaning. It should be emphasized that due to the specific nature of the problems undertaken in this book, it will be the structural (so-called syntactic) methods rooted in mathematical linguistics and classified as artificial intelligence that will be analyzed in depth. The methodology of creating and describing information systems using formalisms of the semantic data interpretation comes in two varieties [9,15,16]:

- the top-down approach—which consists in first considering the most general processes that achieve universality of reasoning and then, in the execution, gradually reaching elementary processes at the lowest level,
- the bottom-up approach—which consists in creating a list of basic events in a given system and a set of elementary processes, and then using them to build more complex processes that reach a high level.

The structural methodology applies to four basic stages in the process of designing an information system, namely:

- Stage I—specifying the requirements,
- Stage II—syntactic analysis,
- Stage III—information system design stage,
- Stage IV—hardware implementation.

The first stage is specifying the requirements. At this stage, the requirements of information system users, the functions that the system should support, and the expectations of its users are described in detail.

The structural analysis stage involves the process of understanding and recording the operating phases of a given system: input, output, data processing, the construction of basic processes, and functions of the information system. The syntactic analysis phase consists of the following stages:

- a system requirement analysis,
- a context diagram of states,
- an entity relation diagram (ERD),
- a mock-up of the user interface,
- a list of processes and a first level data flow diagram (DFD),
- state change diagrams,
- a complete ERD,
- an ERD and DFD comparison,
- a DFD hierarchy,
- a process specification,
- a data library,
- model balancing and documentation.

The end of the analysis stage marks the beginning of the system design stage. At this stage the method of designing the system is identified, taking into account the design of typical systems, custom systems, and the possible adaptation of solutions already known. In addition the application area of the solution developed, which consists of the information system and the model of the system being designed, is defined.

The fourth stage comprises the hardware implementation and adapting the proposed information system for operation.

The structural approach relates not only to the analysis and design of information systems, it is also one of the three approaches from the scope of artificial intelligence techniques used for data interpretation and recognition. The following methods are distinguished in the context of data classification and recognition tasks:

- theoretical/decision-making,
- syntactic-structural,
- neural networks.

The process of creating and designing intelligent information systems is the result of using all the available, known methods and primary components. Primary components include the concepts for describing the information system being created and the methods of its creation. The way the above concepts and methods are selected depends on the system designer, because it is their job to choose those they deem the best and most effective for creating a correctly operating information system.

In late 1990s the class of intelligent information systems started being distinguished within the broader class of information systems [6,8,17]. System intelligence is understood as the system's ability to answer the formulated question in an incompletely determined environment, in conditions of uncertainty, when the right behavior cannot be determined algorithmically but makes success the most likely. Intelligence, with regards to the system operation and the data understanding processes, is built at many levels, called intelligence levels, determined by the following parameters:

- the computing power and the memory capacity of the system,
- automatic searches for data and the automatic selection of its processing routines when the system is used to find solutions to problems which are not completely known at the time the system is built. In this case, system intelligence boils down to:
  - the process of teaching new solutions to the system,
  - adapting new solutions to analysis tasks,
  - modeling the world,
  - generating certain known and expected behaviors,
  - generating situations/cases that are unknown, but can be foreseen,
  - assessing opinions,
  - the linguistic communication,
- the quality and quantity of information collected in the system, both in terms of its semantics and its quantity.

Intelligent information systems are not just to solve specified problems, but also to foresee changes which may take place in the future in order to anticipate the future situation and take preventive action. These systems thus execute the following tasks:

- collecting and storing data,
- interpreting and analyzing information,

- recognizing and understanding data,
- predicting (forecasting) the future situation.

The most important feature of an intelligent information system is the comprehensive and correct analysis of data. How should this notion be understood? The comprehensive and correct analysis of data is an analysis carried out using all the available means, without omitting any of them, in order to determine the most accurate possible meaning of the analyzed situation (data, information). The analysis method is thus a kind of measure of the success achieved. To compare this method using an analogy, various ways of its assessment can be pointed out. However, regardless of the solution adopted, the operation of information systems must aim at satisfying the expectations defined when the information systems were created. These expectations determine the achievement of the defined objective, which directly determines the structure and the tasks of the information system being built. This objective is also used to define the quality criterion, which measures the degree to which the task has been executed. The success of information system operation should be measured on many levels. Intelligent information systems have a very well defined basic quality level of operation and the highest level of achieving success. It is very rare for a system to fully achieve the assumptions made or not achieve them at all. What is much more frequent is a situation in which the system achieves the task to a certain extent, which can be presented in percentages, for instance. What is more, success should be considered a time-dependent variable, because the systems considered most often operate by achieving a given objective in stages.

The operation of intelligent information systems is based on the workings of human intelligence mechanisms which are used to generate certain expectations and beneficial behaviors. Every one of those behaviors relates to the individual capabilities and abilities of functions used to create a given information system. What is particularly important for the correct operation of an intelligent system is to use primary functions which include education, development, and instinct functions. The form of these functions coincides with that of human intelligence functions [15,16] (Fig. 3.3).

Ever information system features a communication function defined in it, used to communicate both inside the system, and also between the system and its environment. The transfer of information between systems or between the system and its environment requires this information to be secured from unauthorized access to it. The information sent is:

- encrypted and sent to the receiver in this form,
- received by the receiver and decrypted,
- interpreted and analyzed by the receiver.

The information interpretation stage should also include the process of its understanding. The process of information interpretation and understanding represents an advantage of intelligent information systems, while the remaining elements of data transmission are characteristic for all information systems.

The operation of intelligent information systems is founded on the complexity theory, whose cornerstones Meystel and Albus [5] saw in the perception, planning, motivation, training, emotions, and knowledge.

The most important component of the foundations of the complexity theory cited by Albus and Meystel is knowledge, which also constitutes the most important element of human intelligence. Processes belonging to the human brain are also characteristic for system solutions. Knowledge

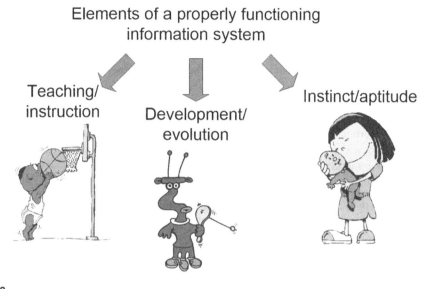

FIGURE. 3.3

Components of an intelligent information system.

resources are found, both in the human brain and also in the "brains" of information systems, in the form of knowledge bases.

The fundamental computational element and at the same time the main component of the human brain is a single neuron. Every neuron is a kind of tiny processor, with receptors called synapses inside. Synapses are located on dendrites. Every message is sent to different neurons located inside the axon, whose every branch ends in a synapse located on a dendrite, in a human body cell far away from other neurons or in a stimulated cell, such as of a muscle or a gland.

Every piece of information received and analyzed is sent to the human brain, where it undergoes an analysis, a classification, and understanding. This is why all stimuli reaching the brain undergo a whole series of processing, interpretation, and analysis routines. Items which characterize given information are extracted from broad information sets using symbols that are assigned to every piece of it. Symbols are a characteristic element of the description in many disciplines and areas of everyday life, such as all known languages, mathematics, science, art, music, dance, and theater. All these areas are based on manipulating one or more forms of a symbolism. It is no different in the case of industry, business, trade, and also military science, which cannot operate without using symbols. The aspects of a symbolic description are due to the lack of the complete understanding of the theory of how neurons in the human brain present symbols or execute various types of operations on the representations.

The aspects of the symbolic description are still a subject of unfinished considerations of science and ongoing research work. All over the world, results of studies based on representations of knowledge are the subject of very active study as part of various disciplines, including informatics. They are a source of lively scientific debate in the fields of cognitive science and artificial intelligence. There is a trend in the group of scientists working on theories defining the tendencies and linguistic representations in the human brain to represent all symbolism as a form presenting logical theories, expert system rules, or linguistic grammars [3,4,6,7,9,10,12,13,18]. Various forms of knowledge representation, among which the most broadly known is the verbal communication, are considered. Apart from this form, also the written form (text), image, and sound are distinguished. Text analysis with regards to its recording in a symbolic form is a task carried out using the phonetic and lexical analyses. Verbal messages are approached similarly, but the form and style of the message must be taken into account (speech analysis). A completely different method applies to describing sound and images. Sound analysis boils down to a signal analysis, a spectrum analysis, identifying and describing the acoustics and the vibrating system which produces certain sounds. When an image is analyzed, it is necessary to describe the variable elements of the image, which may cause different states in different observations.

The fundamental component of the description and characterization as well as the semantic analysis of data is the cognitive science concept, which points out that the human brain is characterized by:

- syntax, which refers to the formal aspect of the information, and
- semantics, which extracts meaning from the information.

Semantic analysis is carried out by intelligent, cognitive information systems, whose main operating principle rests on the aspects of the semantic data interpretation. The semantic information extracted during the description and analysis process, which information reveals the meaning of the analyzed data, allows the significance of the studied information to be determined.

Currently, semantic interpretation and analysis is carried out by advanced cognitive information systems.

The legitimacy of cognitive science theories stems from empirical psychological basis composed of various types of observations. The empirical basis of cognitive science includes the study of reaction times, which shows that various types of intellectual tasks require various amounts of time for people to complete, depending on how complex information processing needs to be carried out. Empirical arguments justifying cognitive science theories also come from the study of Chomsky's generative grammar [15], which is based on the assumption that formal grammatical rules used by natural language speakers resemble those used by a computer—when there are certain logical rules presented—and of a quality similar to that advanced cognitive processes taking place in the human brain.

3.1 DATA PROCESSING

Data processing depends on the type of data analyzed. At this stage of data processing, it is necessary to strive for such a form of its recording that will support its analysis. The most complex form of a data record is an image, because of its complexity and multiobject character. This is because every element of the image should be analyzed individually, but can also be analyzed as a component of a certain whole. In this case, the image is perceived as composed of many objects (multiobject). The multiobject nature of an image may relate to:

- the number of elements making up the given image, of which only selected ones will be analyzed, while the remainder will form a background that is insignificant for the analysis; and
- the number of elements constituting a given image, of which the majority will be analyzed.

If complex and multiobject data is analyzed, the description and analysis process is carried out using a syntactic approach which is rich in the formalisms of linguistic perception and understating of data.

Linguistic data perception and understanding formalisms are implemented using techniques for recognizing and classifying multiobject data (most frequently image data). Data recognition techniques consist of three main groups of data analysis methods [8,9,13]:

- the theoretical/decision-making approach (e.g., statistical),
- syntactic methods, and
- neural networks.

The theoretical/decision-making approach is most frequently used to analyze data which can be presented as feature vectors. In the syntactic approach, data is presented by describing its structure. In the case of data of a complex character, this data is identified with a hierarchical structure made up of simple elements which can be decomposed until primitives are obtained. This is followed by a stage of recognizing the primitives obtained and identifying the relations between them. The structure used to represent data may take one of three forms:

- tree,
- sequence,
- graph.

Depending on the data representation form, various syntactic methods used to analyze it are defined. The following methods are distinguished:

- tree,
- sequence,
- graph.

To represent the image analyzed, the syntactic approach uses formal grammars which include tree grammars, sequential grammars, and graph grammars [9,13].

The process of describing, interpreting, understanding, and semantically analyzing data by using linguistic perception methods is applied in the syntactic approach. The purpose of the analysis carried out is to answer the question whether the analyzed object is syntactically correct for the specific grammar, or not. In the case of a syntactic analysis, the easiest method to use is the sequential method. Sequential languages are used to identify single objects within the analyzed data. Tree and graph languages, in turn, are used to recognize data composed of a greater number of objects (e.g., image, scenes): multiobject data and distorted data. A diagram of syntactic data analysis and its recognition is presented in Fig. 3.4.

Syntactic data recognition consists of the following stages:

- preprocessing,
- image representation, and
- syntactic analysis.

The preprocessing stage covers data acquisition and selection. The data which enables further analysis is selected for the analysis process. Data cannot be incomplete, fragmentary, or illegible. The preprocessing stage consists of filtering, amplifying, approximating, and coding. Then, the data transformation process is executed (in the case of data presented in the image form, for instance). The basic elements of this process are as follows [8,9,13,19,20]:

- binarization,
- segmentation,

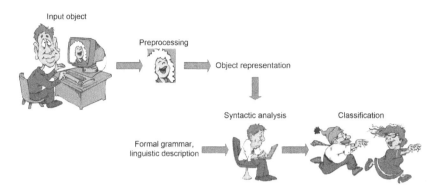

FIGURE 3.4

Stages of the syntactic recognition of objects.

- filtration,
- edge detection, and
- identification of picture primitives and the relations between them.

Every complex object is made up of certain elements which are called primitives. Primitives are the simplest elements which cannot be decomposed into even simpler ones. By identifying the relations between these primitives, it can be determined what the significance of individual elements of the entire analyzed object is and what role they play in the construction of the whole object. The process of segmenting and recognizing picture primitives and the relations between them is based on presenting the image as a hierarchical structure.

The linguistic description is the next stage of the syntactic process of object recognition. This description is drawn up using the description of the elements of the analyzed object and ascribing defining characteristic features to them using the selected grammatical form. This stage consists of the following:

- defining the set of elements analyzed (components),
- describing the pattern to which all the subsequently analyzed objects will be compared,
- identifying relations between the elements of the analyzed object, taking into account the pattern description,
- identifying the dependencies between the elements of the set being analyzed.

After this stage, a formal definition is introduced to the data analysis process. A formal grammar is defined in a form depending on the analyzed datasets. Then, syntactic analysis is carried out to classify the analyzed object. This classification consists in ascribing certain (known) features to the analyzed object. If the system can perform the classification, the object is recognized as one of the objects "known" to the system. If not, the object will not be recognized and the data analysis stage will end in failure. The syntactic analysis stage is used to determine whether a given representation of the object is structurally correct and whether it belongs to the class of objects which can be described using the specified grammar.

This structural analysis is used to match a given pattern defined in the system to the data being analyzed. The degree to which the pattern fits influences the final result of the analysis process conducted, during which the structure of the analyzed image is compared to the structures of pattern images. As a result of this comparison, the analyzed object is recognized by assigning it to the class represented by the pattern which matches it the best.

Syntactic analysis processes are based on sequential methods of image analysis, which include the picture description languages L_{PDL} and the shape feature description languages L_{SFDL} [8,9,13]. The multilevel and hierarchical structure of shape feature description languages L_{SFDL} allows the object to be classified based on a description of its shape in the form of picture primitives, and the features of this shape to be extracted, which process is referred to in the literature as understanding the shape, image, and object. Shaped feature description languages L_{SFDL} identify the essence of the shapes analyzed and are used for the automatic segmentation of multiobject data into quasiconvex or concave areas. This feature leads to the creation of a syntactic description tree of the analyzed objects. An image analyzed at the level of picture primitives is recognized by a deterministic analyzer with a finite number of states and allowing the description of the shape features to be defined at the descriptor level. The shape features of the analyzed image described by descriptors are recognized by a deterministic automaton with a finite number of states [8,9,13].

Syntactic analysis is used to recognize various datasets. If it is supplemented with elements of semantic analysis, it also allows the essence (meaning) of the analyzed datasets to be understood. Such solutions are referred to as semantic reasoning algorithms, which lead to the in-depth cognitive analysis of various datasets. The analysis of the most complex datasets is based on syntax analysis algorithms using the semantic procedures of parsing during the syntactic analysis with the application of, e.g., context free grammars [8,9,13].

This algorithm is based on the operating principles of stack automata, in which the parser reads subsequent structural description symbols (tokens) from the input. These symbols are placed at the top of the parser stack, where they are allocated corresponding values of semantic variables that play a significant role in the semantic analysis process of the reasoning conducted. This process is referred to as the action of shifting another token to the top of the stack (operation: shift). When a so-called handle (i.e., the right side of one of productions) is formed from the group of several recently read terminal symbols, a reduction (operation: reduce) is performed, and as its result, all elements are grouped and at the same time replaced at the top of the stack with a single non-terminal symbol taken from the left side of that production. The next element is that a semantic action defined for a given production occurs during the reduction operation. In that case the operation of the parser aims at reducing the entire input sequence of individual symbols of the syntax analyzer software implementation to just one non-terminal symbol—the start symbol of the grammar—by performing the shift and reduce operations. Parsers based on the above method of operation are called bottom-up parsers. This type of parsers is represented, e.g., by the class of parsers for *LR*(1) grammars or their subclass—*LALR*(1) grammars. As it often happens in practice that the analyzers discussed do not perform the reduction operation if the right side of one of the productions is at the top of the stack, it is then necessary to take into account subsequent symbols appearing on the input of the analyzer. In this situation, the next symbol on the input is analyzed, and after this process is finished, further operations take place. This procedure is necessary to conduct a correct syntactic analysis and semantic reasoning, e.g., for certain language sequences found in programming languages. When the next symbol of the software interpretation of the syntax analysis appears on the input, the parser does not shift that symbol to the top of the stack. It leaves it there for the so-called preview, as a result of which the parser can freely make the number of reductions at the top of the stack necessary to perform the shift of the aforementioned element. This phenomenon is not a rule in the operation of the parser, but only an implication depending on the type of token viewed and leads to a delay in the application of several rules. This will happen if a conflict arises between the shift and reduce actions, as a result of which the parser reduces the expression found at the top of the stack, or shifts the next token from the input to the top. Such a conflict is routinely resolved by giving priority to the shift operation, unless the grammar author has used the appropriate precedence operators [6,9,13].

Another type of conflict is a reduce/reduce conflict which occurs if there are no obstacles to using two or more productions of the grammar to reduce the expression found at the top of the stack at that moment [6,9,13].

The correct operation of semantic reasoning and cognitive analysis algorithms is largely due to the correct work of the parser algorithm. Consequently, it is important to ensure that the fewest possible conflicts occur and to indicate the right class of analyzers used during the entire process of cognitive analysis [6,9,13].

3.2 DATA RECOGNITION AND UNDERSTANDING

Data recognition is a process of the automatic analysis of data which is to answer the question what the analyzed datasets and objects represent. This question can be answered in various ways, ranging from a simple description analysis to the analysis of the features and characteristics of the datasets studied. Recognition is a process similar to the human recognition process. When we look at an object we know what it represents—what it is—or we have completely no knowledge of what we are seeing. The greater our general knowledge, the more elements we can recognize. The situation is similar in the computer data recognition process. The broader the system knowledge bases and the more knowledge the system has of the analyzed data, the more precise the description of the analyzed datasets. The basis for this type of analysis is the syntactic analysis described in the previous Section 3.1. In the data recognition process, an important role is played by semantic analysis, which, apart from the stages of the preliminary data processing, data representation by identifying primitives and the relations between them, also includes the following stages:

- linguistic perception,
- syntactic analysis,
- pattern classification,
- data classification,
- feedback,
- cognitive resonance,
- data understanding.

The main stages of the data recognition process and the semantic analysis are shown in Fig. 3.5. The majority of the semantic analysis stages relate to the process of data understanding. Beginning with the syntactic analysis conducted using the formal grammar defined in the system, the entire analysis process includes stages aimed at identifying the semantics of the analyzed data. The semantics of data is understood as its meaning. The recognition process forms the basis of subsequent analysis stages, namely the cognitive analysis stages.

The data understanding process features feedback, during which the features of the analyzed data are compared to expectations which the system has generated. The system generates those expectations using the expert knowledge base that it has. As a result of comparing the characteristic features of the analyzed data with the expectations generated by the system, cognitive resonance occurs. It reveals feedbacks which indicate the consistency of features and expectations, which are the ones that are significant for the analysis being conducted. In the process of data understanding, the meaning of the analyzed data is identified based on the semantic information contained in the datasets (Fig. 3.5).

The traditional data analysis is performed by defining the characteristic properties of the analyzed datasets. This process is used to take the decision, which is the end result of the data analysis process carried out (Fig. 3.6).

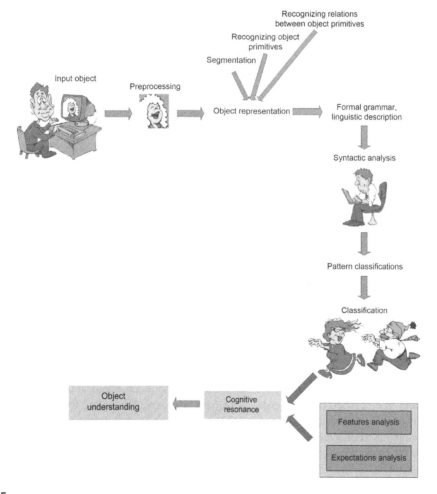

FIGURE 3.5

Data understanding process.

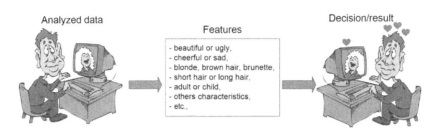

FIGURE 3.6

Process of data analysis.

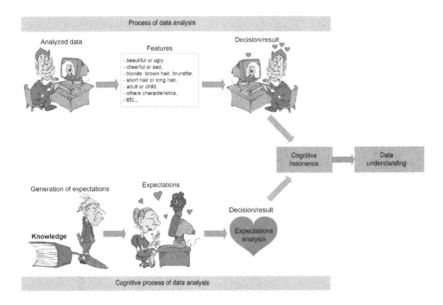

FIGURE 3.7

Data understanding process in cognitive data analysis.

If the data analysis process is supplemented with semantic analysis, which consists in finding pairs of characteristic features and expectations, both consistent and inconsistent, it allows the data understanding process to be carried out. The pairs of features and expectations are found in the process of generating sets of features characteristic for the analyzed data and the expectations produced using the expert knowledge base collected in the system confronted with the analyzed data. Finding consistent pairs becomes the basis of the cognitive analysis process, i.e., the understanding of the meaning of the datasets analyzed (Fig. 3.7).

Semantic analysis carried out in cognitive systems has become the core of the operation of semantic data analysis, interpretation and reasoning systems because of the way in which it is performed as well as the linguistic perception algorithms based on grammar formalisms that are used in its course.

3.3 **CLASSIFICATION PROCEDURES**

Classification procedures of semantic data analysis systems are aimed at the correct assignment of the appropriate patterns and the semantic description to the information sets analyzed. Every data/information set is assigned to the appropriate group of patterns which it resembles the most. This similarity is determined by analyzing the characteristic features of the data/information being described and the characteristic features assigned to the patterns [6,8,9,13]. This situation is presented in Fig. 3.8.

In image recognition processes, traditional decision-making rules implemented using minimum distance methods assume that the unknown object will be assigned to the image to which the object of the training sequence located closest to it in the feature space belongs [6,8,9,13]. This situation is presented in Fig. 3.9.

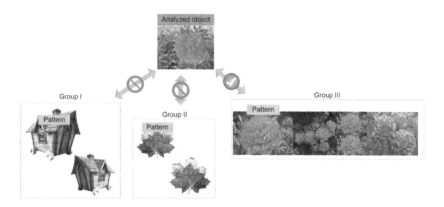

FIGURE 3.8

The process of identifying similarities between the analyzed datasets and a pattern.

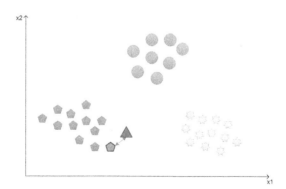

FIGURE 3.9

Assigning an unknown object to an object located closest to it.

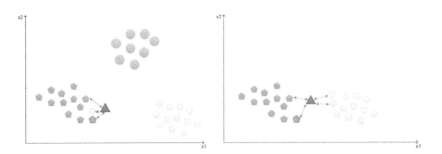

FIGURE 3.10

Assigning an unknown object to objects located closest to it.

The analyzed object (shown as a *triangle* in the illustration) is assigned to the group to which the object closest to the analyzed object in the feature space belongs. This process very frequently leads to the incorrect classification of the object because the only criterion determining its classification is where it is located, or more exactly, the shortest distance between the analyzed object and another object defined in the feature space. However the characteristic features of the analyzed elements are not considered.

There is another way of classifying objects is also suggested for the image recognition process. This one prevents errors due to mistakes in the training sequence, but also reduces the sensitivity of the minimum distance methods used [6,8,9,13]. An example of an application of the above method is presented in Fig. 3.10.

In this case the analyzed object is assigned to the group of objects which are also located closest to it. If the groups are not separated, as shown in the first graph in Fig. 3.10, there will be no unambiguous assignment of the analyzed elements to a group. In this case, the analyzed element will be allocated to a group by indicating the shortest distance between the analyzed object and other objects (not always belonging to the same group). In addition the situation presented in Fig. 3.10 means that the object can be classified to different groups, if its distance to those groups is the same or similar. Consequently, this classification method does not unambiguously answer the question which group of objects the analyzed one will be unambiguously assigned to. This is why the analyzed objects cannot be assigned to certain similar groups using minimum distance methods. The classification methods must base on known recognition methods [6,8,9,13], presented in Fig. 3.11.

Syntactic methods are the best in the classification process because their use makes it possible not only to correctly classify the object based on its characteristic features, but also to identify the meaning of the analyzed objects.

The analyzed datasets with their characteristic features must be compared to sets of patterns. Sets of patterns are defined at this stage of designing semantic data analysis systems and are created by experts as system knowledge bases. The features which most fully and most unambiguously describe the analyzed sets are extracted from the set of characteristic features of the analyzed data. These descriptions contain not only a description of the parameters characteristic for the analyzed sets but also semantic information that characterizes these sets. This information represents the most important element of the semantic data analysis process because it is this information that is used to describe the meaning of the analyzed data/situation/information/process, etc.

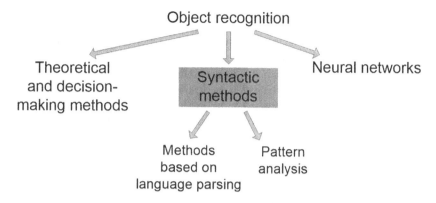

FIGURE 3.11

The classification of object recognition methods.

So how can the consistency between the characteristic features of the analyzed data and the features of the pattern be determined? The more precise the comparison of the features of the analyzed data and of the pattern, the better it is for the process of the semantic data description. This is because it is the level of consistency of the features of the analyzed objects and patterns that determines the "success" of system operation. If the consistency of the characteristic features is poor, the comparison attempts ends in determining no similarity between the analyzed datasets and the pattern defined in the system.

In this situation, the system will be further improved as a result of the process of teaching new solutions to the system, presented in Section 2.4.

3.4 COMPUTATIONAL INTELLIGENCE DESCRIPTION APPROACHES

Artificial intelligence techniques used in the process of analyzing complex data and data rich in semantics as well as designing intelligent information systems of the new generation are now dedicated to various areas of use.

Artificial intelligence and computational intelligence presented in the context of the methods of the semantic description and analysis of data point to various opportunities for applying the methods discussed. The diversity of topical areas of this application is due to the broad range of opportunities for using individual artificial intelligence techniques for data description and analysis processes. Neural networks are the method most broadly known at present. This solution has been presented in the works by Refs. [5,11,14,16]. The approach to the processes of semantic data analysis with the use of linguistic description and semantic interpretation methods is more effective and constantly developed [4,6,7,9,10,12,13].

Data held in information systems is now analyzed in great depth for the purpose of its correct description, interpretation, and processing. Processing very frequently refers to improving data quality, its semantic analysis, recognition, and understanding. The operations of preprocessing, analysis, or classification of the data being analyzed are no longer sufficient in semantic data analysis systems. The data description itself forms the advantage of the "traditional" data analysis systems. The semantic analysis and interpretation of the datasets being analyzed represents a significant process which characterizes "new generation" information systems. The proposal to target information systems at automatically understanding the meaning contained in the sets of data analyzed and processed is raised increasingly frequently. One example of such analysis is the interpretation of medical images or economic ratios.

In the first case, the semantics of the analyzed medical images will have major significance for the diagnosed health of the patient and their future condition. In the second case, determining the semantics of groups of economic and financial ratios will refer to the current and future situation of enterprises or organizations.

Semantic analysis does not apply only and exclusively to the two examples cited earlier. The universality of linguistic methods of describing and interpreting of data means that they can be used in other fields and other applications. The essence of this approach is to adopt what happens in the human mind in computer data analysis tasks. In other words, this process boils down to using solutions which operate by imitating analysis processes executed by the human mind in computer data analysis processes.

In order to conduct a semantic reasoning, made possible by the analysis of various datasets, advanced artificial intelligence techniques are used. These techniques, apart from the simple analysis of information and classification of objects, are designed for extracting significant semantic information which points to the semantic interpretation of data. The semantic analysis of data is embedded in a certain context. This is because it is impossible to simultaneously discover the goal of the analysis and its result.

The process of data understanding is much more complex than the process of data analysis, because in the former process, the information flows from two sources, and in two directions. This makes it similar to the human understanding process. In this model, the stream of empirical data collected and contained in a subsystem designated for recording and analyzing data which is collected and processed in the system according to its purpose interferes with the stream of automatically generated expectations concerning selected features and characteristics of this data. The source of the stream of expectations consists of the resource of knowledge kept in the system which constitutes the base for generating semantic hypotheses, while the knowledge comes from experts who created the knowledge base, from whom this knowledge was acquired and appropriately adjusted for its use in the process of the semantic analysis [10,12,13].

Artificial intelligence and computational intelligence techniques now find their use in cognitive informatics, in which they can drive considerations of semantic data analysis. Their development is dependent on the degree to which cognitive informatics is used for the analysis of diverse data, dedicated to various disciplines of science and applications.

REFERENCES

[1] Andriole KP: Digital image acquisition: computed radiography and digital radiography. In: *SCAR educating healthcare professionals for tomorrow's technology, SCAR University 2001, Society for Computer Applications in Radiology, May 3–6, 2001*, pp 3–6.

[2] Borod JC: Interhemispheric and intrahemispheric control of emotion: a focus on unilateral brain damage. *J Consult Clin Psychol* 60:339–348, 1992.

[3] Ogiela L, Ogiela MR: Visual image biometric identification in secure urban computing. In: Kim TH, Kang JJ, Grosky WI, et al., editors: *4th International mega-conference on Future Generation Information Technology (FGIT 2012), Kangwondo, South Korea, 16–19 December 2012, Computer applications for bio-technology,*

multimedia, and ubiquitous city, communications in computer and information science, vol. 353, 2012, pp 374–380.

[4] Ogiela L, Ogiela MR: Cognitive systems for intelligent business information management in cognitive economy. *Inter J Inf Manag* 34(6):751–760, 2014.

[5] Meystel AM, Albus JS: Intelligent systems—architecture, design, and control, Canada, 2002, A Wiley-Interscience Publication John Wiley & Sons, Inc.

[6] Ogiela L: Computational intelligence in cognitive healthcare information systems. In: Bichindaritz I, Vaidya S, Jain A, et al., editors: *Computational intelligence in healthcare 4: advanced methodologies, studies in computational intelligence*, vol. 309, 2010, pp 347–369.

[7] Ogiela L: Towards cognitive economy. *Soft Comput* 18(9):1675–1683, 2014.

[8] Duda RO, Hart PE, Stork DG: Pattern classification, New York, NY, 2001, A Wiley-Interscience Publication John Wiley & Sons, Inc.

[9] Ogiela L: Cognitive computational intelligence in medical pattern semantic understanding. In: Guo MZ, Zhao L, Wang LP, editors: *4th International Conference on Natural Computation (ICNC 2008), Jian, China, 18-20 October 2008, proceedings*, vol. 6, 2008, pp 245–247.

[10] Ogiela L: Cognitive informatics in image semantics description, identification and automatic pattern understanding. *Neurocomputing* 122:58–69, 2013.

[11] Zadeh LA: Fuzzy logic, neural networks, and soft computing. *Commun ACM* 37(3):77–84, 1994.

[12] Ogiela L: Semantic analysis and biological modelling in selected classes of cognitive information systems. *Math Comput Model* 58(5–6):1405–1414, 2013.

[13] Ogiela MR, Ogiela L: Cognitive informatics in medical image semantic content understanding. In: Kim TH, Stoica A, Chang RS, editors: *1st International conference on security-enriched urban computing and smart grid, Daejeon, South Korea, 15–17 September 2010, Security-enriched urban computing and smart grid, communications in computer and information science*, vol. 78, 2010, pp 131–138.

[14] Pratt WK: Digital image processing, New York, NY, 1991, Wiley & Sons.

[15] Chomsky N: Language and problems of knowledge: the Managua lectures, Cambridge, MA, 1988, MIT Press.

[16] Kickhard M, Terveen L: Foundational issues in artificial intelligence and cognitive science, Amsterdam, 1996, Elsevier.

[17] Huang HK: Picture archiving and communication systems in biomedical imaging, New York, NY, 1996, VCH Publishers, Inc.

[18] Ogiela MR, Ogiela U, Ogiela L: Secure information sharing using personal biometric characteristics. In: Kim TH, Kang JJ, Grosky WI, et al., editors: *4th International mega-conference on Future Generation Information Technology (FGIT 2012), Kangwondo, South Korea, 16–19 December 2012, Computer applications for biotechnology, multimedia, and ubiquitous city, communications in computer and information science*, vol. 353, 2012, pp 369–373.

[19] Brejl M, Sonka M: Medical image segmentation: automated design of border detection criteria from examples. *J Electron Imaging* 8(1):54–64, 1999.

[20] Minsky M: A framework for representing knowledge. In: Winston P, editor: The psychology of computer vision, New York, NY, 1975, McGraw-Hill, pp 211–277.

THE FUNDAMENTALS OF MANAGEMENT SCIENCES

Management theory is currently understood as a science on the interface of economics and humanities. This is because it skillfully combines these aspects of the above disciplines which allow the decision-making process to be directly streamlined and which optimize all of its components. The two-way nature of this type of approach has become very natural because the correct operation of diverse processes is driven both by the economic basis for their optimization and by problems from the sphere of humanities. In addition the second type of problems is constantly extended. The influence and significance of psychology, sociology, or philosophy is identified within the context of the development of management theory [1–3]. Fundamental questions thus arise: How to manage effectively? What to manage? What should be the result and the effect of this process?

The answers to these questions are not unambiguous, because they depend on the entirety of the situation, phenomena, environment, etc.

In this book, the reader's attention will be drawn to the topics of the semantic (cognitive) management of information and data [4–6]. In order to be able to answer the question about the semantic analysis of data in the management processes, it is necessary to refresh basic problems related to it.

Management processes discussed in this book will concern information management tasks. Information management is a very complex task today. The complexity of this problem should be understood not as an extreme complication of a process which is based on the execution of complex tasks, but as a process which is the sum of many different subprocesses. The tasks associated with the process of the correct management of information pose challenges concerning data processing and analysis, and are considered to be some of the hardest tasks among all the currently known management problems. It is thus worthwhile considering what this difficulty results from.

Firstly, it relates to defining what information and knowledge that can be used if selected information is available really is. The difficulty also results from detailing the essence and the meaning of information and knowledge in decision-making processes. In this regard, information will be understood as the primary element, a kind of component of the entire knowledge process. Knowledge, in turn, will be understood as a notion which presents a given information in a deeper perspective. To compare these two concepts, their following characteristic features are distinguished:

- Information:
  - is static in nature, may be enriched with additional aspects,
  - is independent of the entity, which means not dependent on any person, institution, organization, etc.,
  - is overt in the case of public information or secret in the case of confidential information,
  - may take any form and shape,

- is this simplest, basic element of knowledge,
- may be copied,
- may have meaning (semantics).
- Knowledge:
  - is dynamic and growing in nature,
  - is dependent on the entity,
  - is overt, publicly accessible, but if his knowledge refers to secret information, its availability is restricted,
  - may take any form and shape,
  - is built from the information held and its meaning,
  - may be distributed,
  - its meaning depends on the situation which it concerns.

Information is thus a component of knowledge, while knowledge is made up of information, experience, observations, skills, and meanings.

What is extremely significant is the way the knowledge is used, the unambiguous identification of the intentions for which the information held is used, as well as the methods of using it. Knowledge which will be used for cognitive, scientific, and interpretation purposes will be easy to define and identify. Definitions will consist in the simple identification of unknown (undefined) concepts, situations, and cases. From this perspective, knowledge will be addressed to all its potential recipients. At the time knowledge will become generally accessible, public, understood, of broad utility. However, if the knowledge is used for unethical purposes, there will be a problem with even defining it. In this case, it is difficult to state unambiguously that layers of knowledge have been used. This is because the earlier example refers to an ethical contradiction, wherein knowledge which is perceived as an element of the ethical world can be used for unethical purposes. To the extent to which this is an example of using knowledge elements or layers, it is difficult to demonstrate that in such cases information also determines knowledge. This example shows that knowledge may be used in various situations, environments, and ways. It is, therefore, important what purpose information, data, and messages constituting elements of the knowledge are used for. Who uses the collected knowledge held and for what purpose? Who do the results of the knowledge used concern or refer to?

A similar note applies to identifying, defining, and sourcing knowledge in any organization. So how should knowledge be acquired? How should knowledge already collected be used? In what case should the arcana of the knowledge held be used?

Decision-makers are constantly struggling with answers to such questions. Individuals taking decisions and responsible for analyzing the various situations occurring in an enterprises, organizations, and institutions constantly improve techniques of the correct analysis and taking of decisions [7–9]. However, answering these questions does not yet guarantee that the organization will operate correctly. The efficient management of knowledge collected guarantees the correct growth of the company. In management processes, knowledge is understood as the correct use of all available, reliable information about the past, present, and future situation of the company, its environment, the reasons for the current situation, and also the ability to project the future state. Knowledge accumulated at various levels of an organization or institution allows management processes to be improved, but only that collected at the highest level, i.e., the strategic decision-making one, allows the organization to be managed effectively because it enables the intellectual capital of the organization to be consolidated.

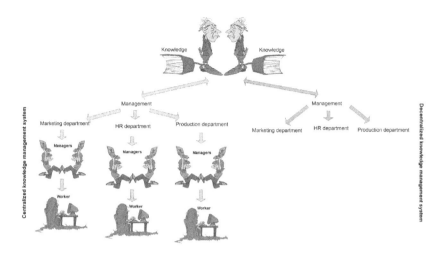

FIGURE 4.1

Knowledge layers in knowledge management systems.

The process of collecting knowledge is a basic, primary stage in knowledge management. In knowledge management processes it is important to use the collected knowledge correctly. The correct use of knowledge depends on the system of its handling existing in the entity and people will use it. IT systems for knowledge management which improve management processes differ depending on whether the knowledge is centralized or decentralized. In every system, it is important that information be transferred efficiently and reliably. If information is distorted or omitted, the entire knowledge management process becomes useless. Information transferring significantly improves the process of its utilization, but does not guarantee the correct use of information for the tasks that are executed. This is because the effectiveness of this process depends only and exclusively on the correct analysis of the data held.

In traditional knowledge management systems, layers of information form an element supporting corporate management (Fig. 4.1).

Fig. 4.1 shows the process of acquiring knowledge in a centralized and decentralized knowledge management system. In both cases, managers gain the most complete knowledge possible in order to collect the complete information about the company situation, its environment, competitive conditions, the drivers of the current and future company success, the reasons for its failure, etc. However, there are differences in the way that knowledge is transferred in a centralized and decentralized system. Knowledge is transferred between the remaining elements of the entire system, which is composed of individual departments and employees. The differences in ways knowledge is transferred are mainly due to the design and type of organizational structures to which they are dedicated.

In a centralized system, knowledge forms one of many elements of the entire management process, whereas in a decentralized one, it constitutes one of few elements of the entire system. Consequently, in knowledge transferring processes, it is better to use decentralized systems as they pose a lower risk of possible distortions or errors at each stage of knowledge transfer.

Knowledge management processes do not concern solely the methods of collecting knowledge, processing it and using it to improve the operation of the organization. Obtaining knowledge from generally accessible information resources implies the use of information management processes including the following topics [4,10–13]:

- planning, designing, and implementing an information strategy,
- the information flow in external communication,
- the information flow in internal communication,
- ensuring investment financing for developing and implementing new IT solutions,
- the correct use of available IT solutions,
- information quality management,
- ensuring data security,
- ensuring training and development of the IT staff and system users,
- the ability of the company to effectively interact with the information market,
- integrating information systems used at various levels.

Information management processes precisely indicate directions in which knowledge management process support will be used to secure strategic information.

4.1 DECISION PROCESSES IN MANAGEMENT SCIENCES

Decision-making processes carried out when executing tasks of data management take place in different entities with different frequencies. These processes are found not only in enterprises and organizations, but also in various structures and entities as well as in everyday life. Decisions are taken incessantly, during the analysis of more or less complex processes, but every one of them ends in the decision-making stage. Decision-making processes can differ in:

- the level of difficulty of solving them,
- the topical area they concern,
- the time necessary to carry out further analysis,
- the use of computation algorithms,
- the need to apply automatic solutions and information systems.

An analysis of decision-making problems is also dedicated to supporting management processes. Data management processes:

- apply to various information sets, ranging from information of low importance to information that is strategic or secret,
- concern information contained in numerical sets, signals, sounds, images, biometrics, etc.,
- relates to sets composed of various amounts of information—from small quantities of information to large, extensive datasets forming broad databases.

Regardless of how different the analyzed sets of data/information are, the methods of managing this type of information must be determined.

The most widespread methods of managing information have been described in the publications [4,5]. These methods focus on the optimal execution of all possible information processes occurring in any structure. This process consists in:

* executing control tasks at the stage of data acquisition,
* creating information sets,
* analyzing datasets,
* storing information,
* providing unprocessed ("raw") data and information obtained during the analysis process,
* sending information inside the structure in which it is collected and outside that structure.

At the data acquisition stage, information undergoes data collection and recording processes. At this stage, the greatest possible amount of information from all accessible sources is obtained. At this time, the information collected is not analyzed with regards to its suitability for the analysis process to be carried out. Not all of the acquired information will be significant for the analyzed dataset, and its significance will be confirmed at the stage of data selection. It will then be determined which of the information collected in the system is important and indispensable for the analysis process to be carried out, and which turns out to be superfluous. Significant data is separated from insignificant data at the next stage of the information management process.

At the stage when datasets are created from the information collected, a process is carried out to extract data of significance for the analyzed aspect, information set, or process. The essence of this significance is also an element of the analysis process. The significance of the analyzed data may be very high, moderate, or low. Significant data that is semantically associated with the main element of the analyzed datasets should be extracted from the entire information set as the most important in the entire process. The remaining elements of this set are stored for the purpose of their possible future analysis. At this stage, the elements of the information/datasets to be analyzed should be fully consistent with the following:

* the defined data analysis method,
* the subject of the analysis,
* expectations about the information assessment process to be carried out,
* the nature and significance of the elements of the set undergoing the analysis.

After the stage of data acquisition, collection and preselection carried out by determining its significance for the analysis process to be conducted, the next stage in the information management processes is data analysis. The data analysis stage is the broadest of the processes forming part of data management. During data analysis, the following is done:

* defining and selecting the analysis method,
* preliminarily assessing the analyzed sets,
* assessing components (individual data and information) and their meaning,
* indicating success factors and the causes of failures,
* projecting the future state.

The data analysis process itself can be varied. Datasets can be described and assessed with regards to:

* the type of data,
* the nature of the analyzed data,

- the significance of the analyzed information,
- the impact of data on specific phenomena,
- the development or stagnation of the analyzed situation, etc.

In the presented perspectives on the processes of data analysis, this selection of data description, assessment, and analysis methods is ambiguous and depends on the tasks executed and intended. At the data analysis stage, an assessment and an analysis of information sets subjected to these processes takes place. However the data description process itself is not sufficient to correctly evaluate the analyzed situation or phenomenon. In this case the results obtained must be evaluated by verifying conclusions. This process becomes the starting point for the reasoning stage, which is important for assessing the studied phenomenon in the future, i.e., for the projection process. The reasoning stage thus includes a projection process aimed at:

- foreseeing the future state of the analyzed phenomenon,
- assessing the possibility that the specific situation will occur in the future,
- assessing the reliability of the projected situation.

Based on the analysis results obtained at every one of the earlier data analysis stages, an information set forming the final result of the process carried out is created. The information obtained at this stage and combined with the datasets is stored. The essence of the data storage process is to secure the collected information and the data analysis results obtained from being disclosed to unauthorized and third persons. If the collected data is confidential, secret, or strategic in nature, it can be protected from disclosure using the appropriate information protection, security, and concealment algorithms [10–15]. This process is about securely storing data and is connected with the next stage in data management, i.e., the stage of sending information and making it available.

At this stage, information is secured during the following processes:

- data transfer and sending among the remaining information recipients,
- processing data to make the contents of the information held available,
- decrypting encrypted information if the access to it has been verified successfully.

The process of making confidential or secret information available is about giving individuals, groups of individuals, institutions, computer systems, etc., who are allowed to use information sets access to them. At this stage of the data management process, the party trying to obtain information sets is verified by confirming their compliance. In the case of secret data, the verification stage is understood as the confirmation of the compliance of the persons attempting to assess the encrypted datasets. If the verification process is successful, full access to the collected data and its sets is granted. If the verification fails, information sets are not released to a given entity.

The data and information collected in the information system constitutes the most important element at all stages of the information management process. Their processing, evaluation, analysis, storage, and future use means that processes of managing sets of information used for various purposes and in various ways are constantly carried out.

Processes of data management are aimed at processing data to such an extent that the information can be used in the optimal way.

Hence, data management systems are most frequently used to efficiently collect data, process it, and store it. Intelligent information management systems are supplemented with cognitive data analysis. In information management systems, semantic analysis leads to the process of understanding the data being analyzed, the reasons for the phenomena occurring and assessing the situations that may occur in the future. This is because cognitive analysis is used to determine the meaning of the analyzed information sets. In information management systems, it is carried out on the basis of the description, and the interpretation of the semantic contents collected in the analyzed datasets. Cognitive analysis makes it possible to assess whether the analyzed data is of major importance for the development of the analyzed entity or not. It thus allows the unambiguous elimination of those aspects of the analysis process which are of no major importance for the development of the enterprise or organization.

Ensuring the security of semantic data analysis systems used to support management processes is therefore of major importance for the secure process of managing information. Security, strategic, and financial data is particularly sensitive.

Information management system security is developed by applying cognitive analysis in management systems and cryptographic algorithms to ensure the security of data collected in the system.

Semantic data analysis systems and information security systems belong to the group of cognitive systems. This class of systems has been described in publications [5,6,8,9,16] which presented their characteristic features and the drivers of data management processes at enterprises.

Information management processes in traditional data management systems comprise the following stages:

- collecting sets of data/information,
- data analysis—an analysis of the entity's operations,
  - economic analysis,
    - financial analysis,
      financial standing of the entity,
      asset situation of the entity,
      revenues and expenses,
      cash flow,
    - technical-economic analysis,
      production volumes,
      tangible fixed asset value,
      employment levels,
      material management,
      technical and technological progress,
  - environment analysis—in a holistic perspective, in a detailed perspective, and of the relations between the enterprise and its environment,
- the use of the collected information,
- data storage.

Unlike traditional information/data management systems, data management processes running in intelligent, cognitive information management systems comprise the following stages:

- acquiring and collecting information/data by accessing information from the following sources:
  - in-house data collected at the entity,
  - data obtained from the outside,

- semantic analysis of strategic (important) data:
  - data analysis based on the interpretation of the semantic aspects of the analyzed information,
- semantic reasoning,
- future standing evaluation—prediction from analyzed data.

Cognitive systems supporting decision-making processes are dedicated to the semantic analysis of data and the improvement of data management processes.

4.2 COMPUTATIONAL INTELLIGENCE IN DATA ANALYSIS IN MANAGEMENT PROCESSES

Intelligent information systems are currently used in every area of research, and increasingly frequently in practice as well. The scope of information system application can be very broad. This class of systems works, among others, in transport, defense, economy, management theory, production, logistics, technology, computer science, or telecommunications.

The correct operation of an intelligent information system rests on two planes, namely [4,6,17]:

- identifying repeatable activities found in information processing, and
- identifying informationally and algorithmically complex decision-making processes, which represent the key processes executed by the information system.

The information flow in intelligent information systems, which accounts for all unexpected events, is ensured by collecting a large volume of data/information whose size and type depends on the decisions taken and which constitutes an element of the entire information/decision-making process. The key elements of this process are as follows:

- planning the necessary subprocesses occurring in the entire information/decision-making process:
  - projecting the future state,
  - planning processes within different time cross-sections and horizons,
- planning the additional subprocesses that may occur in the entire information/decision-making process:
  - projecting the future situation that may occur,
  - planning processes that may occur within different time cross-sections and horizons,
- coordinating all the necessary and additional subprocesses, events, and operations that may occur in the information/decision-making process,
- monitoring and controlling the course of all operations in the entire information/decision-making process,
- the operational steering of information processes, particularly the collection, processing, and transfer of data.

Information logistics systems, which are aimed at improving the management of resource flow processes to satisfy the needs of all participants of logistics processes and customers represent an example of information systems. Key elements of information management processes in this class of information systems include:

- integrating systems for the shared use of the resources held, taking the form of:
  - integrating the data held,

- integrating the applications developed and used,
- network and system integration,
- unifying the component functions of such systems in order to unify the functions executed by the system,
- access of all organizational units to the database in order to ensure efficient access to the information held,
- broadly deploying visualization methods to support the processes of analysis, decision-making, projecting future states, transferring information, and analysis results.

Logistics information systems are used to collect and process data related to the logistical activities of the enterprise as well as the data obtained from the macro environment, with particular emphasis on the operations of the competitors. Data of this type is obtained from various sources, both overt and covert. In addition, logistics information systems are responsible for providing the data acquired and collected in knowledge bases to teams that take decisions at every organizational level. The solutions used in logistics systems produce benefits by improving the customer service system and material management by:

- shortening delivery times,
- reducing inventory levels,
- optimal forecasts of the analyzed states and situations,
- improving the ability to use just-in-time strategies and marketing strategies.

Solutions adopted to correctly execute tasks in logistics information systems are supported by methods working based on [4]:

- controlling production according to the MRP II—Manufacturing Resource Planning standard,
- MRP II Plus, MRP—Money Resource Planning—an extension of MRP II standards by adding financial procedures, i.e., cash flow, ABC—Activity Based Costing method,
- ERP—Enterprise Resource Planning, ERP II, and also
- comprehensive quality management.

Navigation is also used in the construction of information systems, because it plays a major role in executing transport processes, e.g., when the transport is characterized by a wide distribution of the rolling stock. The use of navigation systems optimizes the processes of dispatching, transporting, and moving goods as well as the ability to determine their precise location at every stage of the whole process.

Individual information systems are increasingly frequently identified with modules of an integrated management information system (IMIS). The basic features of integrated management systems include [4]:

- a high level of integration of all data held and processes executed,
- a modular design,
- system openness,
- a comprehensive functional nature,
- advanced business knowledge,
- the use of state of the art technologies,
- the functional and structural flexibility of the solutions implemented.

The design of integrated management systems is based on individual types of subsystems which form the components of the IMIS. Basic components of integrated management systems are shown in Fig. 4.2.

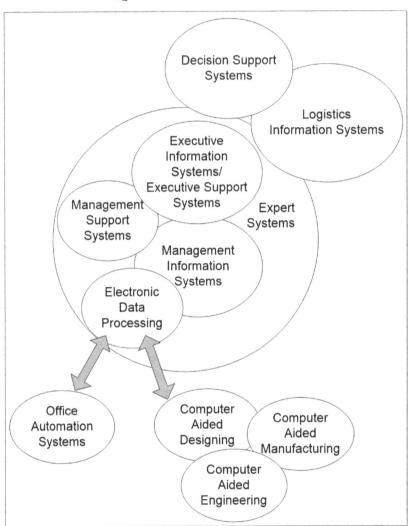

FIGURE 4.2

Integrated data management systems.

Fig. 4.2 shows the components of integrated data management systems in the form of all the available types of information management systems. In addition the relations and links present within this system have also been shown. The most important components of integrated data management systems include [4]:

- Transaction Processing Data Systems—TPS or Electronic Data Processing—EDP,
- Management Support Systems—MSS,
- Management Information Systems—MIS,
- Executive Information Systems—EIS, frequently treated as Executive Support Systems—ESS,
- Expert Systems—ES,
- Decision Support Systems—DSS,
- Logistics Information Systems—LIS,
- Artificial Intelligence Systems—AIS frequently implemented as Artificial Neuron Networks—ANN,
- Office Automation Systems—OAS,
- Computer Aided Designing—CAD,
- Computer Aided Manufacturing—CAM,
- Computer Aided Engineering—CAE.

The components of an integrated information management system connect fully and complement one another so that they constitute its obligatory parts, without which the correct operation of the entire system would not be possible.

Management information systems constitute one of the basic management systems. These systems give the entity a marketing, technological, organizational, and functional advantage in the environment in which the entity exists. The main purposes of this information system are to provide the necessary, up-to-date, and consistent information to the group managing the company. The information is available at every level of the enterprise/organization which allows its correct and efficient operation. This operation ensures the execution of the plans adopted and their compliance with the needs, which may change over time. It also takes into account the managerial capabilities of the managerial staff and account for the variable, unstable market situation.

Management information systems are designed and built in a way that guarantees the security of the data collected and processed. In addition, this data must be protected at every stage of system operation. This is ensured by the restricted and authorized access to information. The scope of management information systems covers the following:

- the plans of the entity,
- current information,
- necessary tables and reports,
- exchange of instructions and decisions,
- new proposals and initiatives,
- all opinions and intentions,
- discussions of current matters and problems, and
- proposed meetings, training, discussions, projects, and workshops.

Management information systems are used to support decision-making processes, coordinate tasks executed by the entity, and improve the work performed.

Another class of information management systems comprises quality assurance systems, which relate to the holistic operation of the unit and ensure the production of high-quality software used in information systems. This class of systems does not operate independently, because they form a part of the information system with an embedded quality assurance system.

The main factors which drive the improvement of product or service quality include:

- employee engagement in the quality assurance process,
- materials used to improve quality,
- technologies used to ensure quality improvements,
- methods used to improve the state.

Quality assurance systems are based on engaging company management in quality improvement processes. This engagement, combined with the will and contribution of the employees, the purchase of new technologies, the improvement of the quality of materials used by the organization, the use of better methods of organization and production related to the operational systems applied by the given entity can ensure the improvement of its quality.

Trading organizations also used trade information systems. This solution ensures the correct, timely, and necessary exchange of information between production facilities and trading units of the vendor/customer type. The main task of this type of systems is to shorten the manufacturer—vendor—buyer cycle.

Trade information systems analyze information concerning:

- the goods and services offered,
- sales and warehousing processes,
- the trading partners of the given entity, namely manufacturers, vendors, and competitors.

Trade information systems comply with the just-in-time principle not only with regards to the task of delivering goods, products, or services, but also in the sense of delivering components necessary to produce the final product. This class of systems is used to ensure the correct operations related to protecting the data and the security of the transactions concluded. They are used at companies, enterprises, and organizations: among the management, in production, in the marketing and accounting departments, in the sales and design departments, and also in relations with customers and banks, in

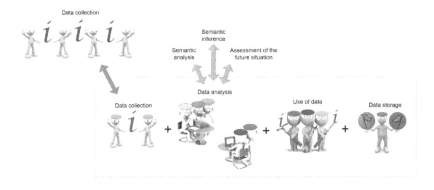

FIGURE 4.3

Cognitive analysis aspects in management systems.

particular in the process of financing the operation of the organization. Trade information systems are used in trade, banking, finance, but also in defense.

Another class of systems comprises spatial information systems whose purpose is to:

- ensure the secure exchange of information between airports and aircraft,
- provide information about every aerial object and zones in which specific objects are located,
- enable airport staff to react to potential emergency situations,
- simplify agreements between air carries and the management of airfields or airports,
- prevent present and projected threats.

A decisive role in spatial information systems is played by time as the element strategic for the optimum operation of this class of information systems. Spatial information systems are an example of hybrid systems created by a combination with real-time systems.

Another example of information systems is provided by geographical information systems. Their main purpose is to present, record, store, and analyze local or global geographic information. They are used for geographic analyses carried out to economic, environmental, but mainly defense ends. In addition, they indicate development directions for spatial information systems in relation to systems handling information about a given area and the ability to manage traffic.

The most important type of information systems are decision support systems which are used in every area in which information systems operate. This group refers to the stages and processes of the operation of complex information systems, associated with the need to take decisions. Every decision-making process is characterized by the existence of many premises and the complex logic of the entire analysis process. Decision-making systems are found in all types of organizations, enterprises, institutions, structures, and every place where the process of taking strategic and key decisions is complex, multilateral, multistage, conditional on time or access to data information as well as the access to state-of-the-art technologies. Decision-making support in information systems consists in:

- the rapid and full access to large sets of information,
- the ability to semantically and deeply analyze the data held,
- the ability to visualize the data collected in the system, its processing and determining its meaning,
- the semantic interpretation of the analyzed datasets,
- modeling the situations, phenomena, or areas of reality that appear and are described,
- accounting for expert knowledge in the form of a set of rules contained in the IT system,
- extending expert knowledge sets by including new solutions,
- automatically teaching new solutions to the system.

Information systems include various classes of systems. They are used to improve the processes occurring in social and economic life, as well as in strictly scientific solutions. There is often no clear border between applications of various classes of information systems. This is why information systems require the actions of many entities, in the various areas of their operation.

The use of the semantic description of the analyzed information sets is characteristic for cognitive systems that support data management processes.

Cognitive information management systems analyze data by interpreting its meaning. In this regard, this class of systems deploys computer intelligence processes to analyze data. The traditional data management processes have thus been supplemented with elements of cognitive analysis (Fig. 4.3).

Executing the semantic analysis in information management systems makes it possible to determine the characteristic features of intelligent systems that support data/information management processes in an enterprise/organization/any entity. This class of systems not only manages strategic/important/secret data, but mainly semantically interprets the analyzed information.

Cognitive systems for semantic data analysis which support data management processes are used to intelligently manage information by supplementing this type of processes with elements of computer data understanding. These processes are used to:

- send information to the appropriate units/entity,
- directly identify the causes of a situation that occurred (whether good or bad),
- eliminate the "hot potato" forwarding of information between the wrong units,
- immediately react to eliminate the causes of the poor condition of the unit/entity.

Semantic layers of the analyzed datasets, extracted from the sets of data which undergo analysis, determine its significance and meaning in the entire interpretation and analysis process. Hence, cognitive analysis serves to extract features that are significant in data analysis processes.

REFERENCES

[1] Branquinho J, editor: *The foundations of cognitive science*, Oxford, 2001, Clarendon Press.
[2] Ekman P: Facial expressions and emotion. *Am Psychol* 48:348–392, 1993.
[3] Schachter S, Singer J: Cognitive, social and physiological determinants of emotional state. *Psychol Rev* 63:379–399, 1962.
[4] Laudon KC, Laudon JP: *Management information systems – managing the digital firm*, ed 7, New York, NY, 2002, Prentice-Hall International, Inc.
[5] Ogiela L: Data management in cognitive financial systems. *Inter J Inf Manage* 33(2):263–270, 2013.
[6] Ogiela L, Ogiela MR: Management information systems. In: Park JJ, Pan Y, Chao HC, et al., editors: *2nd FTRA international conference on Ubiquitous Computing Application and Wireless Sensor Network UCAWSN, South Korea, 07–10 July 2014, Ubiquitous computing application and wireless sensor, lecture notes in electrical engineering*, vol. 331, 2015, pp 449–456.
[7] Ogiela L: Advanced techniques for knowledge management and access to strategic information. *Inter J Inf Manage* 35(2):154–159, 2015.
[8] Ogiela L, Ogiela MR: Efficiency of cognitive information systems supporting enterprise management tasks. In: Barolli L, Palmieri F, Silva HDD, et al., editors: *9th International conference on Innovative Mobile and Internet Services in ubiquitous computing IMIS 2015, Brazil, Blumenau, 08–10 July 2015*, pp 166–170.
[9] Ogiela L, Ogiela MR: Comparison of cognitive information systems supporting management tasks. In: Xhafa F, Barolli L, editors: *International conference on Intelligent Networking and Collaborative Systems INCoS, Taiwan, Taipei, 02–04 September 2015*, pp 49–56.
[10] Ogiela L: Intelligent techniques for secure financial management in cloud computing. *Electron Commerce Res Appl* 14(6):456–464, 2015.
[11] Ogiela L: Cryptographic techniques of strategic data splitting and secure information management. *Pervasive Mob Comput* 29:130–141, 2016.
[12] Ogiela L, Ogiela U: Information security in intelligent data management processes. In: Barolli L, Xhafa F, Ogiela MR, et al., editors: *10th International conference on Broadband and Wireless Computing, Communication and Applications BWCCA 2015, Poland, Krakow, 04–06 November 2015*, pp 169–172.

[13] Ogiela MR, Ogiela L, Ogiela U: Security in management of distributed information. In: Park JJ, Pan Y, Chao HC, et al., editors: *2nd FTRA international conference on Ubiquitous Computing Application and Wireless Sensor Network UCAWSN, South Korea, 07–10 July 2014, lecture notes in electrical engineering*, vol. 331, 2015, pp 457–462.

[14] Ogiela L, Ogiela MR: Bio-inspired algorithms in data management processes. In: Xhafa F, Barolli L, Messina F, et al., editors: *10th International conference on P2P, Parallel, Grid, Cloud and Internet Computing 3PGCIC, Poland, Krakow, 04–06 November 2015*, pp 368–371.

[15] Ogiela MR, Ogiela L: Bio-inspired approaches for secret data sharing techniques. In: *ICIIBMS 2015 International Conference on Intelligent Informatics and Biomedical Sciences, Japan, Okinawa, 28–30 November 2015*, pp 75–78.

[16] Ogiela L, Ogiela MR: Semantic data analysis algorithms supporting decision-making processes. In: Barolli L, Xhafa F, Ogiela MR, et al., editors: *10th International conference on Broadband and Wireless Computing, Communication and Applications BWCCA 2015, Poland, Krakow, 04–06 November 2015*, pp 494–496.

[17] Zadeh LA: Fuzzy logic, neural networks, and soft computing. *Commun ACM* 37(3):77–84, 1994.

COGNITIVE INFORMATION SYSTEMS

5

Cognitive information systems have been proposed as a subclass of intelligent information systems, which carry out both a classical data analysis based on data processing and interpretation routines, and an in-depth analysis understood as a detailed one aimed at understanding data and reasoning based on it. This kind of analysis is carried out using the semantic information (content) held in sets of the information processed, or more precisely, in the layers of knowledge found in the analyzed datasets [1,2].

An information system analyzing various data and information, where this analysis is executed based on defined features characteristic for the analyzed sets, has knowledge collected in its knowledge bases [3]. This knowledge is necessary for the complete and correct analysis of data, and at the same time forms the basis for generating the system's expectations concerning the analysis carried out by it. Identifiable and describable characteristic features of the analyzed data are combined with the expectations generated by the system and concerning the semantic contents of the analyzed data. Then the system tries to compare them. During this stage, the degree of consistency of the characteristic features and expectations, or of their inconsistency, is determined [2,4].

Cognitive information systems are designed based on a structural reasoning technique to match the patterns defined in system knowledge bases. A system cognitively analyzing data can do this with various types of data recorded in different formats: numerical, image, etc. [1,5,6]. In order to match data to patterns, the analyzed datasets are compared to the pattern defined in the system, which represents each type of the analyzed data in the most accurate way. This comparison is carried out by establishing strings of derivative rules which allow this pattern to be generated. The pattern, as the most accurate reflection of the analyzed datasets in which all characteristic features are recorded, is used to determine a kind of similarity between it and the remaining elements of the set. This determination of the level of similarity is understood as the correct identification of the element, which takes place when the analyzed element is compared to the pattern characteristic for the set. Every element of the set undergoes a comparative analysis, and if similar features are identified, the element is recognized correctly. If not, the element will not be recognized because of the lack of similarity between it and the defined pattern (Fig. 5.1).

The process of recognizing and understanding data by way of the above comparison is founded on strings of derivative rules, calls productions, defined in the formal grammar introduced. This formal grammar defines the formal language which supports the process of semantic data analysis. The set of data recognized during the semantic analysis is assigned to the class to which the pattern that represents it belongs [7].

Cognitive Information Systems in Management Sciences. DOI: http://dx.doi.org/10.1016/B978-0-12-803803-1.00005-7

FIGURE 5.1

The process of recognizing the analyzed elements of the set by comparing data to the pattern element.

Cognitive data analysis borrows the methods of describing and interpreting the analyzed sets from the syntactic approach. For the purposes semantically describing the analyzed sets, this approach uses functional blocks. During the stages of preliminary data processing, which include—depending on the form of data—coding, shape approximation, filtering, processing data on the system's input, it is possible to obtain any representation of the analyzed set, for instance in the form of hierarchical semantic tree structures in subsequent steps of deriving this representation from the initial symbol of the introduced grammar.

When preprocessing the data they analyze, cognitive systems also perform (depending on the type of that data) its segmentation, they identify primitives and point out relationships between these individual primitives.

The correct classification of data leads to recognizing whether the given representation of the analyzed information belongs to the class of data generated by the formal language defined by the proposed formal grammar.

Data interpretation processes aimed at its cognitive analysis are more complex than data recognition processes. This is because the recognition process is to ascertain whether the analyzed object is known the system and whether the latter can recognize it or not. In contrast, semantic processes are to recognize the element together with all the determinable factors that condition is form, i.e., to define the determinants of a given state (past, present, and future) concerning the analyzed data. The semantic data analysis process is complex and two-way. Its two-way nature stems from the process of data description and interpretation, during which the system independently collects knowledge and describes the analyzed datasets.

5.1 **DEFINITION OF COGNITIVE SYSTEMS**

Cognitive systems have been proposed in publications [1,2,8], which introduces the definition of this class of systems.

Cognitive systems were defined as systems that "describe intelligent information systems designed for conducting in-depth data analyses based on the semantic contents of the data. Semantic analyses are conducted with algorithms for describing this data based on processed expert information (for example in the form of knowledge bases) and the processes of machine (computer) perception and understanding of data performed, e.g., using mathematical linguistics" [1,2,8].

Cognitive systems are thus used to semantically interpret and analyze various sets of data, if these sets contain layers of semantic information. These layers, in turn, are used to describe the semantic context of the analyzed data. What is the semantic context? The semantic context should be understood as the entire information contained in the analyzed datasets and in information external to that analyzed, but which refers to it directly. All information concerning the reasons of phenomena, situations, the determinants of the future behavior and the course of phenomena can constitute the semantic context. In this sense, the analysis of datasets cannot concern only and exclusively the information collected in these datasets, but must primarily be based on information outside of them. This is why expert knowledge bases play a major role in cognitive systems. This type of bases is used to collect broadly understood expert knowledge which is significant for the correct analysis of data. This knowledge, taken from various sources, allows the data to be described and used for reasoning. Reasoning processes constitute a characteristic element of the constantly executed semantic analysis. Today, data cannot be analyzed without taking into account its changes caused by the passage of time.

Cognitive information systems are used to analyze various datasets [4,9–11]. Because of the different nature of the sets analyzed, cognitive systems have been classified into six basic types:

- Understanding Based Decision Support Systems,
- Understanding Based Image Analysis Systems,
- Understanding Based Management Support Systems,
- Understanding Based Person Authentication Systems,
- Understanding Based Signal Analysis Systems,
- Understanding Based Automatic Control Systems.

All the types of cognitive information systems presented before have wide-ranging applications, from management and economics, sociology and philosophy to technical, military, and defense sciences, medicine, natural and biological sciences [1,8,12–14].

Subclasses defined according to the type of data analyzed are distinguished within each cognitive system class. The classification of cognitive systems is still open because the changes of the world around us imply the need to account for new areas in which semantic analysis is necessary for their correct assessment [15–17].

All cognitive system types use methods of cognitive analysis in their operation to extend the capabilities of classical data analysis technologies in order to reason based on the semantics (meaning) of the analyzed data or information.

The characteristic features of the cognitive systems discussed here are as follows [1,2,8]:

1. a broad spectrum of analyzed data—cognitive information systems can analyze various data, because the cognitive methods based on cognitive resonance which are implemented in the system are universal,

2. wide-ranging opportunities to use cognitive information systems in various scientific fields,
3. the use of formalisms and tools from the area of informatics which support semantically-oriented cognitive reasoning with the use of structural artificial intelligence techniques,
4. the use of the unity of cognition and action rule—the idea behind the operation of cognitive systems is to implement human cognitive processes which are used by cognitive information systems, but at the same time combine these cognitive processes with the action which cognitive systems execute at their last operating stage, that is at the stage of determining the directions of subsequent activity,
5. the use of knowledge bases made up of the appropriate expert knowledge collected,
6. accounting for the chronometries of systems which are based on the chronometry methods of the mind, i.e., determining the reaction time for analyzing a given phenomenon in relation to the stage of transmitting information about the analyzed data to the system, the stage at which the system processes this information and the stage at which the cognitive system programs the reaction and executes it,
7. the ability to deploy cognitive information systems taken from the scientific research domain in the practical solutions.

Cognitive information systems are used to understand and semantically analyze different types of data. Their significant feature is that as a result of the analysis of data conducted by the system, this data can be semantically interpreted and analyzed. This type of data description and analysis allows semantic information to be extracted, which makes it possible to reason at the stage of the data analysis conducted.

5.2 HUMAN PERCEPTION MODELS IN COGNITIVE DATA ANALYSIS AND DECISION-MAKING

In computer processes of data analysis, and also of decision-taking, it is beneficial to use perception models characteristic for the human mind. The essence of this solution is to use algorithms which can be transferred to the domain of system solutions in automatic analyses of data. The more complete this transfer and acquisition of information about how certain cognitive tasks are performed in order to use it in computerized data analysis, the more accurately the system imitates the human mind. Of course, there are no system (computer) solutions that are completely convergent with the operation of the human mind, but these two processes of analysis coming from the different worlds are constantly becoming more similar.

System solutions are modeled, among others, on solutions that describe the operation of the material world, on determining the significance of matter and energy in this world and defining information and intelligence. Models of this type go hand-in-hand with solutions, which identify the operating rules of the human perception and become the foundation for building cognitive solutions used to analyze and take decisions based on understanding a given situation.

Human perception models used for cognitive data analysis tasks which support decision-making processes include [7]:

1. *The model of information representation in the human brain*—This model shows that every piece of information which reaches the human brain is stored in the form of a specific representation.

This representation is unambiguous and unambiguously assigned to a given piece of information. All information representations are:

- individual—for every person and computer systems constructed by them,
- unique—in their mind, every individual assigns different representations to different pieces of information (Fig. 5.2).

Information recorded in any form, e.g., of sentences, words, strings of characters, images, situations, events, and the like, reaches the human brain where its structure is examined. This process is aimed at presenting the information in the human brain. This information undergoes processing routines that can

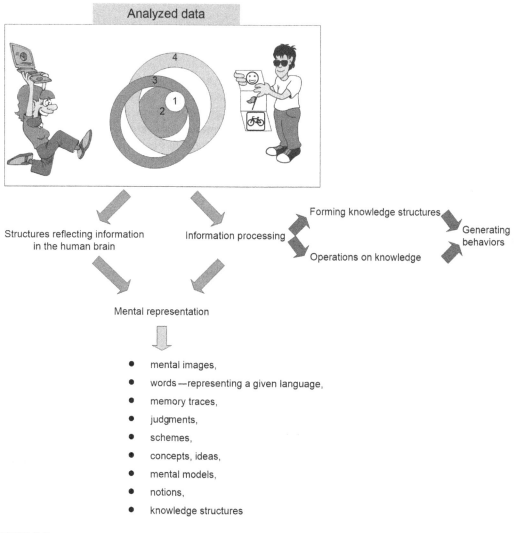

FIGURE 5.2

Cognitive information representation model.

be executed using the knowledge possessed by the individual. This is a type of acquired knowledge. Then, knowledge structures are created, and these structures, when combined with certain expectations, generate specific behaviors. This set of generated behaviors is used to record the information in the form of a selected mental representation. These representations can take various forms, e.g.:

- mental images,
- words—representing a given language,
- memory traces,
- judgments,
- schemes,
- concepts and ideas,
- mental models,
- notions,
- knowledge structures.

2. *Neural informatics model (NeI)*—This is a solution which focuses on the structure of human neurons and points out similarities between the human and computer processes of data interpretation and description. This is a biological/psychological view of the ways in which knowledge and information are represented in the human brain. These representations are located at the neural level and are portrayed using mathematical models. Neural informatics constitutes a field of cognitive informatics within which the human memory is described. This memory is seen as the foundation of both natural and artificial intelligence.

3. *Cognitive informatics model*—Based on the identifiable and describable similarities in the structure of the natural, human mind, and its corresponding artificial "mind." In this model, elements of the human mind used for cognitive tasks are linked to their artificial counterparts built by cognitive informatics. Mental processes characteristic for humans, namely perception, memory, thinking, data analysis and interpretation, reasoning and predicting, are transferred to the field of computer science solutions to construct cognitive robots and machines. For a human, the design of a cognitive model resembles the structure of a block cognitive/decision-making system, whereas for a computer, the structure of its artificial counterpart.

4. *Cognitive computer models*—Created by combining three main components:
   - artificial intelligence,
   - cognitive science, and
   - system applications and solutions (Fig. 5.3).

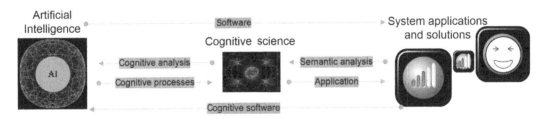

FIGURE 5.3

Cognitive computer model diagram.

These primitives, with the connections and relations between them, make up models of cognitive computers. Models of cognitive computers are created by combining cognitive solutions from the field of artificial intelligence in which natural intelligence processes adopted for machine analysis purposes are identified, and cognitive processes which form the basis for the semantic analysis of data. System applications are developed using the solutions adopted in the artificial intelligence area. Cognitive computer models activate natural intelligence processes to distinguish the correct solutions and the right cognitive structures. Semantic analysis processes are executed by cognitive solutions, which form the foundation of applied solutions. Artificial intelligence also influences the design of software, which forms a part of the applications developed.

5. *Models of cognitive machines*—Models were designed by combining three components which include:
- artificial intelligence,
- cognitive science, and
- system applications and solutions (Fig. 5.4).

All components of the model, with the connections and relations between them, make up solutions referred to as cognitive machines. Cognitive machines are robots used for various tasks connected with the occurrence and execution of cognitive processes. They are most frequently humanoid robots or artificial brain structures. Cognitive machine models are created by applying cognitive solutions to artificial intelligence tasks and activating processes of human intelligence to identify the optimum cognitive solutions and structures. In addition, semantic description processes are adopted to execute cognitive solutions, which form the basis of the applications that are developed. Artificial intelligence models are used to construct control mechanisms, which form the components of the solutions designed.

The models of human data perception and analysis, which are based on executing cognitive processes, are used not only in the data analysis process, but also in those improving decision-making. In the case of cognitive systems, decision-making processes are understood as the type of processes that help take optimum decisions based on an in-depth analysis of the problem—i.e., data understanding. This process is extremely complex, and the solutions of this type are best illustrated by humanoid robots which, when executing the tasks entrusted to them, analyze the situation and take a decision about executing actions similar to those performed by a human. Of course, the execution of these actions depends on the intelligence of the specific robot as well as the ability to teach robots new behaviors and taking decisions which they didn't know before. Hence, these are solutions that depend on the situation, are previously unknown and offer new opportunities for development.

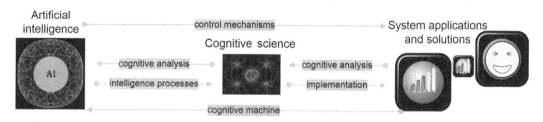

FIGURE 5.4

Cognitive machine model diagram.

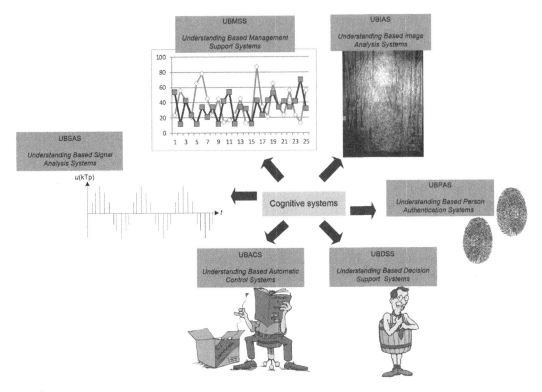

FIGURE 5.5

Cognitive systems classification.

5.3 TYPES OF COGNITIVE DATA ANALYSIS SYSTEMS

Cognitive system classification is open because new areas in which semantic data analysis systems can be used are constantly found. Primary classes of cognitive information systems deal with decision-making, image and personal analysis, and supporting decision-making processes [7,15,18–20].

Semantic data analysis based on learning about and understanding the studied phenomenon has now offered an opportunity for developing intelligent information systems almost in every field in which data is analyzed. A general classification of cognitive information systems, which use cognitive analysis processes for semantic interpretation and reasoning, is presented in Fig. 5.5.

Cognitive information systems include, among others, Understanding Based Decision Support Systems—UBDSS [7]. Systems of this class are designed to support decision-making processes and use them for reasoning, while these processes are executed based on semantic data interpretation. Decision-making processes, as the foundation for the operation of the majority of information systems, are designed to take optimal decisions in the most efficient way. In this sense, their role is to optimize decision-making processes.

In the classical view of the decision theory, systems supporting decision-making processes operated by adapting the behavior of an ideal and perfectly rational decision-maker, who can be either a natural person or a system, to the task of selecting one of a certain number of well-known options. Semantic data analysis systems supporting decision-making processes operate based on the utility principle. This means that they analyze options that produce certain benefits from taking the right decision. In addition, this class of systems takes the set of all decisions that can be taken and rejects those that are not realistic, and which are less likely to occur than others.

Cognitive systems supporting decision-taking should have the fullest and broadest knowledge of all decisions that can be taken and are available to the system (the possibilities of the system). The overwhelming majority of decisions are taken in conditions of risk and uncertainty. The risk most often stems from taking decisions based on incomplete knowledge, without knowing certain significant data, and determinants of the analyzed condition, etc. In such situations, there is the risk that an error will be made in the entire decision-making process. Minimizing the likelihood of this situation occurring is the key task in the decision-making process. The smaller the risk of committing an error by taking the wrong decision, the more certain the decision taken.

Cognitive systems supporting decision-taking are developed to conduct analyses during which the system considers all the options that can occur and compares their suitability in every regard. This comparative analysis is carried out by the decision system within a specified time and defined computing capacity. These components imply taking the optimal decision within the optimal time. Otherwise the system would conduct a decision-making analysis for a time exceeding that of common-sense solutions.

Semantic data analysis systems analyze within an optimal time, based on the ability to analyze and process the solutions available to them and assess every option. A situation in which the system would have all cognitive resources seems to be impossible because collecting the complete information about every available solution is unlikely. Acquiring the broadest possible set of information about the options that can be taken as well as considering and analyzing every one of them is possible only in the case of large and robust teams.

In semantic data analysis systems, the decision-taking support is provided by assigning the degree of importance to the decision criteria adopted. Every decision criterion that is considered is assigned a weight, because some of them are more important than others. In addition, selected decision criteria can be considered only if they are linked to other criteria, so they cannot be considered as independent solutions.

Decision-making processes are characterized by:

- optimization of the solutions adopted—concerns the analysis and assessment of all solutions that can occur,
- decision-taking speed—concerns the time it takes to execute the decision-making process,
- economy—concerns the complexity and the level of difficulty of cognitive operations performed as part of the decision-making process.

An important role in the decision-making process is, therefore, played by the heuristic of:

- "follow what is most important"—in this case, decision-making is based on the principle of following criteria, each of which has a different level of importance, and the most important one is selected. The selection of the most important criterion makes it possible to compare individual options in pairs. As a result of this comparison, those of them whose importance is lower or unknown are rejected.

- the rule "follow what worked last time"—this criterion refers to taking decisions based on the solutions that worked out in the last attempt of the same type. This is a comparative criterion related to the previous successful solutions. However, it eliminates the solutions that have not been found to be optimal in previous comparative processes.
- the perspective theory—which defines the impact of the mental representation of the analyzed decision-making task on the content of the decisions taken. Cognitive representation of a decision-taking problem may undergo a partial or a complete change as a result of the effect of the methods and words used to describe it, or as a result of selecting a broader context of the decision-taking process under consideration. As a result of executing the decision-taking task, a kind of frame (restriction) is imposed on the situation considered. This means that the problem is presented from a certain defined perspective (restricted by the frame), and then the decision is taken which complies with the framing process. This type of solution is right only if the defined frame fully portrays the analyzed problem. If the analyzed problem is incorrectly restricted, the decision-making process will also contain errors.

Cognitive decision-making systems are built by reference to all the identifiable and definable elements of the human decision-taking process. Not all stages and components of human decision-taking processes can be transferred to system (computer) solutions. Cognitive decision systems are designed using elements of psychological theories transferred to the field of information systems. The cognitive decision-making process, in turn, is an attempt to reflect and imitate the operation of the complex psychological process containing components from the scope of cognitive and motivation tasks.

The classification of cognitive systems also distinguishes Understanding Based Management Support Systems (UBMSS) designed for supporting management processes with the use of various types of data, e.g., ratios, strategic information, planning information, etc. [2,3,21]. In this group of cognitive systems, an important role is played by information aspects of a strategic nature and relevant to the analyzed situation. These aspects refer not only to the stage of acquiring and collecting data but also to the stages of its correct processing, analysis, and interpretation. This class of systems, just like other types of cognitive information systems, operates by semantically analyzing data. In addition the cognitive process operating as part of the information system makes use of the semantic web phenomenon present in the semantic web model. In cognitive models, concepts connected with decision-making systems are permanently stored in the form of a hierarchical web structure made up of nodes and relations identifying the links between these nodes. In particular nodes of the network, various concept representations are coded, and features characterizing these concepts are identified. These features are assigned to concept representations at the lowest possible level of generality. Defining the correct conceptual representation complies with the principle of cognitive operation economy. This means that the economy of the web structure is most often connected with the cost of its operation.

Semantic data analysis systems execute the processes of analyzing, interpreting, and reasoning, which allow data collected in knowledge bases (whether this data is collected in the system or is publicly available) in which the conceptual representations are coded to be used in the optimal way. In cognitive information systems which support data management processes, the semantic web includes the concepts coded in the system, presented in the form of nodes of the network, and semantic relationships that define the links between individual nodes. The semantic relationship between the conceptual representations is the sum total of all connections that can be traced between their designates and properties. Closely related concepts are characterized by a number of interconnections in the network, corresponding to the set of all features. These connections are called web patch and should be differentiated in cognitive systems according to their weights. This means that the stronger the connection between defined conceptual representations, the greater the weight assigned to the path connecting these concepts. This solution produces a simpler activation in the process of information analysis. When designing cognitive management systems, the duality of semantic relationships between concepts should be kept in mind. This duality means that relationships are built on positive connections and also along negative paths. Building relationships by determining positive relationships is aimed at identifying the greatest possible number of consistent (positive) links and references, and eliminating cases where there are no links or the relationships are negative. Semantic relationships defined based on negative paths are used to determine the semantic distance between conceptual representations. Their feature is therefore indicating that sentences positively connecting the represented concepts are false. Semantic web models thus allow semantic relationships between conceptual representations to be identified.

Semantic Web models can be used to construct cognitive personal authentication and verification systems, i.e., UBPAS (Understanding Based Person Authentication Systems) [13–15]. This class of systems analyses personal data using biometric identification processes. These systems are based on the direct and indirect ways in which memory works.

In the direct methods, the system recalls all information about which it has knowledge from its memory. This is thus an example of processes oriented at recalling knowledge. In addition, in the set presented to it now the system recognizes all elements that were present in a previously applied or learned set. A system for the semantic analysis of personal data also classifies data, analyses it, interprets it, and reasons about it. UBPAS systems operate using the data collected in sets of overt and covert knowledge. The system analyses datasets about which it has certain knowledge (these sets have been analyzed in this system before), and new information/data fulfilling definition criteria previously unknown to the system. If data unknown to the system is analyzed, the system does not reveal the definition of the analyzed information/data, while it classifies and identifies elements which fulfill the adopted definition or which do not. The existence of covert knowledge sets can be detected based on the following criteria:

- The exclusivity criterion—The selected analysis method refers only to the knowledge resources necessary for executing the current task. When certain processes of semantic analysis are executed, only data that is independent of other elements of the set and at the same time not related to the execution of the task is used.
- The sensitivity criterion—The type of analysis carried out allows the complete, properly classified information collected in the system knowledge base to be revealed. If the system has incomplete knowledge, it cannot treat the remaining knowledge as covert. If complete overt knowledge cannot be collected in the system because, for instance, it is impossible to collect, this may not be treated as equivalent to the remaining knowledge being covert.

In the case of semantic data analysis systems, it is difficult to separate overt knowledge from the covert one. In this class of systems, a significant role is ascribed to overt knowledge bases, which can be influenced by covert knowledge, semantic information contained in the sets of analyzed data and which is extracted from the entire dataset. Hence this is an example of covert knowledge which is extracted using certain mechanisms of data description and processes of its analysis.

The next class of semantic data analysis systems are cognitive systems referred to as UBIAS (Understanding Based Image Analysis Systems) used to analyze data in image form [1,4]. One development within this class of cognitive systems consists in systems for supporting the understanding of various medical images which represent some of the most complicated image data. Numerous, varied sets of image data have been semantically analyzed. They include the images of:

- the central nervous system, the spinal cord,
- metatarsus and foot bones,
- wrist and hand bones,
- long bone fractures.

UBIAS systems proposed by the author for the purpose of analyzing medical images are intensively developed, with research conducted on the semantic analysis of varied images of lesions of various human organs and body parts [1,4].

The semantic analysis of medical images has been applied to analyzing the following X-ray images of:

- spinal cord,
- metatarsal and foot bones in three different projections:
  - dorsoplanar,
  - external lateral,
  - internal lateral,
- the wrist and hand bones,
- long bone fractures of the upper extremities.

UBIAS systems were used to semantically analyze all the above classes of medical images.

The first class of UBIAS systems are cognitive systems for spinal cord analysis.

An analysis of spinal cord images was proposed to determine the regular structure of the central nervous system, namely the spinal cord, and detect possible deformations of this organ. The semantic analysis of this class of medical images allows the following deformations to be detected:

- spinal cord widening,
- cysts,
- cancerous tumors:
  - extramedullary,
  - intramedullary,
- spinal cord structures and compressions,
- degenerative lesions.

The proposed semantic analysis of the detected deformations and lesions allows the current and future condition of the patient to be assessed. The assessment of the analyzed lesions is supplemented with information about the reason why the deformations occurred, their size, number, and changes that can occur in the future.

The second class of UBIAS systems are cognitive systems designed for the semantic analysis of foot bone images have been defined for the tasks of analyzing foot bone deformations and pathologies, in particular for analyzing [1,4]:

- various types of foot bone fractures,
- degenerations leading to skeleton deformations,

- bone displacements,
- the appearance of an additional bone among foot bones,
- the appearance of hematomas, calcifications, and various irregularities in the structure of foot bones.

The semantic analysis in cognitive systems dedicated to description and analysis of foot bone images was proposed for different projections in which medical data/images of metatarsal bones are acquired the dorsoplanar projection, the external lateral projection, and the internal lateral projection.

The semantic analysis of metatarsal bone images has been extended to include the analysis of foot bone images by including toe bones in the semantic description of foot bone images. An cognitive analysis of foot bone images was proposed with reference to possible lesions and deformations, which include [1,4]:

- toe and foot bone fracture,
- degenerative lesions,
- deformations of foot bones,
- arthritis,
- tuberculosis of bones.

The types of deformations are very typical for foot bone pathologies. For performed analysis, it was especially selected foot bone fractures, foot deformations, and pathologies as arthritis or tuberculosis, as a typical foot bone lesions.

A detailed description of the solutions proposed for the semantic analysis of foot bone images, including the introduction of definitions of grammars and formal descriptions that are to support the semantic analysis, interpretation and description of analyzed data in the image form, has been dedicated to cognitive analysis of many kinds of food deformations.

The next example of cognitive systems dedicated to semantic analysis of medical data, is the UBIAS systems dedicated to hand bone analysis. UBIAS systems designed for the semantic analysis of hand bone images have been defined for the tasks of analyzing hand bone deformations and pathologies, in particular for analyzing:

- finger fractures,
- hand bone fractures,
- degenerative changes (bone fusions or bone atrophy),
- hand deformations,
- bone displacements,
- arthritis,
- tuberculosis of bones.

A detailed description of the solutions proposed for the semantic analysis of wrist and hand bone images, including the introduction of definitions of grammars and formal descriptions that are to support the semantic analysis, interpretation and description of analyzed image data, has been dedicated to cognitive analysis of many kinds of hand deformations.

The next example of cognitive systems dedicated to semantic analysis of medical data, is the UBIAS systems for long bone fracture. Cognitive information systems designed for analyzing images showing fractures of long bones of upper extremities have been proposed for various images of long bone fractures, which include [1,4]:

- oblique fractures,
- transverse fractures,
- spiral fractures,
- longitudinal fractures,
- comminuted fractures,
- fractures after which a part of the bone has not returned to the correct position relative to the other part—a displaced fracture.

Linguistic formalisms have been used in UBIAS systems for the semantic analysis of various image data. An assessment of the utility of semantic analysis methods for image data has shown that the solutions introduced for the purpose of cognitively analyzing and interpreting data are correct.

The next classes of cognitive information systems are the extended UBIAS systems—E-UBIAS systems. The systems for the semantic analysis of different medical images have been extended to include:

- the processes of the individual/personal description with biometric analysis of analyzed data,
- the process of image data analysis with a stage of system learns new solutions.

The first example of E-UBIAS systems for the semantic analysis of data is the solution by adding description and interpretation processes based on biometric features—individual, personal features—made it possible to semantically analyze extended datasets. This kinds of cognitive analysis dedicated to the individual/personal and semantic description of data was implemented by combining the cognitive analysis of hand bones with the biometric features. This analysis was carried out by defining individual sets of hand geometry features and biometric traits. This kinds of data description proposed for the cognitive analysis of selected medical data and the biometric analysis of the hand, including the introduction of definitions of sets which can be used to carry out any extended analysis of individual/personal features, has been dedicated to cognitive interpretation and analysis of image data [1,7].

E-UBIAS systems proposed for a personal analysis are also very useful in defining individual sets of minutiae in combination with the cognitive description and identification of the structure of hand bones. Defining sets of characteristic minutiae in the cognitive analysis provided the opportunity to extend systems for the semantic analysis of medical images by adding personal features [9,14].

The second example of E-UBIAS systems is the cognitive information systems, which are learning new solutions. The new approach to personal and cognitive data description and analysis was implemented by adding stages of learning new solutions not yet defined in the system's knowledge base to the semantic analysis of foot bone images. This analysis was carried out after adding new, formerly unknown elements to knowledge bases. This stage of the biometric analysis was used in the process of the cognitive analysis of data, after the process of personal identification as well as personalization was added to this stage. The introduction of the biometric analysis offers great opportunities for extending cognitive information systems because biometric, individual features which increases the accuracy of assigning a person to the set of analyzed data can be added to all processes of cognitive data interpretation and analysis.

All the classes of cognitive information systems presented earlier are characterized by a broad spectrum of applications, ranging from management theory, economics, sociology, and philosophy to engineering, mathematics, medicine, and Earth science [10,12,16,17,21–23].

The operation of all types of cognitive information systems is founded on the use of cognitive analysis methods which significantly extend the capability of classical data analysis techniques. This process leads to reasoning based on the data description and the use of its meaning, i.e., the semantics of the sets.

5.4 COGNITIVE DATA UNDERSTANDING SYSTEMS

Cognitive data analysis systems execute data understanding tasks. What does the data understanding process mean? The process of understanding data is the most accurate possible identification of the meaning of this data. This accuracy results from the description and interpretation methods used. The more accurate methods are used to describe the data, the more complete this process, which means that the data will be described more precisely. The description of data is used for its interpretation. The interpretation process may end in a simple description of the data contained in the sets described, or, much more beneficially, may contain information about the reasons for this situation occurring. This process is the starting point for the data understanding stage. The ability to define the reasons why a certain phenomenon occurs, what its characteristic features are, and assessing their future state based on their full analysis is referred to as understanding. This means identifying a certain sense of the occurrence of a given state, situation, value of sets, course of processes, etc.

The execution of analysis processes understood as above is characteristic for cognitive information systems, which describe, interpret, and understand the semantics of data. Cognitive information systems are designed to semantically interpret data. It is this feature that distinguishes them from the remaining classes of information systems. The characteristic features of this system class are as follows:

- a broader range of data they analyze can be identified—cognitive information systems are used to analyze various types of data,
- the data interpretation and analysis methods implemented are universal,
- the opportunities of using cognitive information systems in various fields of science and practical applications are broad,
- linguistic formalisms tailored to semantic cognitive reasoning tasks are used,
- structural techniques of artificial intelligence can be used,
- there are broad possibilities to implement cognitive processes characteristic for human thought processes in the tasks of semantic data description and interpretation,
- the results obtained through implementing cognitive processes can be combined with reasoning processes, e.g., at the stage of defining the directions of further research,
- unlimited use of expert knowledge bases collected in cognitive systems is possible,
- theoretical solutions introduced for cognitive information systems can be applied in the domain of practical solutions.

Cognitive date understanding systems are designed for extracting semantic information and determining its meaning for the entire analysis process. Hence their most important job is to determine the impact of the layers of semantics contained in this sets of analyzed data on the current and future state. The capabilities of assessing this impact are varied because they result from the level to which the analyzed data is known (the amount of knowledge held about the analyzed data), from the solutions adopted for the analysis problems, from the available time and expert knowledge, from the hardware capacity and access to it. However the most important aspect of analysis processes is the knowledge held about the meaning of the analyzed data.

5.5 DECISION PROCESSES IN COGNITIVE SYSTEMS

The processes of describing, interpreting, and analyzing data executed by cognitive information systems are aimed at understanding the analyzed data. The data understanding process is multistage and complex.

The first stage of the data analysis process consists in defining the set of data to be interpreted and analyzed—all the data that will be subject to the description and interpretation processes is collected at this stage. The system uses the collected data to generate a set of features characteristic for the entire set of analyzed data. The set of characteristic features is defined by extracting information which unambiguously describes data (elements of the entire set) from the set of data. Extracting characteristic features is to support an efficient data analysis process. The decision process at this stage makes it possible to take a better decision to indicate the most important characteristic features of the dataset analyzed. During the analysis process, a decision is taken about which features from the set of all characteristic features should be selected for further analysis.

In parallel, a second process is executed as part of the semantic analysis of data carried out by cognitive information systems. The system collects knowledge convergent with the type of data/information it is analyzing. This knowledge is received from experts and collected in system knowledge bases. The knowledge collected in the system is used to generate certain expectations about the analyzed datasets. After those expectations have been generated, the decision-making process takes place. This process refers to helping to take the decision about accepting the generated expectations—from the set of all expectations—for further analysis. In this process, the selection of those expectations which concern the analyzed data to some extent should play an important role. Beneficial solutions are selected based on the convergence of the expectation with the selected characteristic feature(s) identified at the stage of feature extraction. Running the decision-taking process twice is to help take the decision on selecting the right elements from the set of features and expectations which are earmarked and recommended for further analysis. The duality of the decision-making process is due to the fact that it is the identification of the right components which determines whether the entire analysis process will be correct. The decision to accept certain elements for further analysis is taken by assessing the degree of importance of a given element (its meaning) in the entire analysis process. In the process of analyzing economic indicators, the values of specific ratios, the frequency of their occurrence, the magnitude of changes (fluctuations), etc. will be of major importance. In contrast, a low weight should be assigned to, for instance, the name of the company, because it has no impact on the analysis of the value of economic or financial ratios.

As a result of executing decision-making process at this stage of extracting characteristic features of the analyzed datasets and extracting expectations about the analyzed sets, the elements of both sets are combined and compared. Their combination makes it possible to determine whether the elements both sets are consistent, which then leads to the data understanding described above, or inconsistent, which will then result in the lack of understanding of the analyzed data. In the latter case, it is possible to assess the reasons of this situation. If the system has performed the analysis based on incomplete knowledge, then it is possible to train the system. New solutions will be taught to the system on the following basis:

- supplementing datasets with new data,
- adding new knowledge to expert knowledge bases,
- supplementing the set of characteristic features with new features—both for sets of data analyzed during the first attempt to analyze them and for the new, supplemented datasets,
- supplementing the set of expectations with new elements—both for sets of expectations generated during the first analysis attempt and for the new, supplemented set of expectations generated for the supplemented datasets.

REFERENCES

[1] Ogiela L: Cognitive informatics in image semantics description, identification and automatic pattern understanding. *Neurocomputing* 122:58–69, 2013.
[2] Ogiela L, Ogiela MR: Cognitive systems for intelligent business information management in cognitive economy. *Int J Inf Manage* 34:751–760, 2014.
[3] Ogiela L, Ogiela MR: Management information systems. In: Park JJ, et al., editors: Ubiquitous computing application and wireless sensor, lecture notes in electrical engineering 331, Springer Dordrecht Heidelberg, New York; London, 2015, pp 449–456.
[4] Ogiela L, Ogiela MR: Data mining and semantic inference in cognitive systems. In: *2014 International conference on Intelligent Networking and Collaborative Systems (IEEE INCoS 2014), Salerno, Italy, September 10–12, 2014*, pp 257–261.
[5] Branquinho J, editor: The foundations of cognitive science, Oxford, 2001, Clarendon Press.
[6] Grossberg S: Adaptive resonance theory: how a brain learns to consciously attend, learn, and recognize a changing world. *Neural Networks* 37:1–47, 2012.
[7] Ogiela L, Ogiela MR: Semantic data analysis algorithms supporting decision-making processes. In: Barolli L, et al., editors: *10th International conference on broadband and wireless computing, communication and applications, Krakow, Poland, 4–6 November 2015*, pp 494–496.
[8] Ogiela L: Towards cognitive economy. *Soft Comput* 18(9):1675–1683, 2014.
[9] Ogiela L, Ogiela MR: Bio-inspired algorithms in data management processes. In: Xhafa F, et al., editors: *10th International conference on P2P, Parallel, Grid, Cloud and Internet Computing 3PGCIC, Krakow, Poland, 4–6 November 2015*, pp 368–371.
[10] Ogiela L, Ogiela U: Information security in intelligent data management processes. In: Barolli L, et al., editors: *10th International conference on broadband and wireless computing, communication and applications, Krakow, Poland, 4–6 November 2015*, pp 169–172.
[11] Ogiela MR, Ogiela L: Personalized cryptography in data sharing and management. In: Barolli L, et al., editors: *18th International conference on Network-Based Information Systems (NBiS), Taipei, Taiwan, September 2–4, 2015*, pp 269–272.
[12] Ogiela MR, Ogiela L: Bio-inspired approaches for secret data sharing techniques. In: *ICIIBMS 2015 international conference on intelligent informatics and biomedical sciences, Okinawa, Japan, November 28–30, 2015*, pp 75–78.
[13] Ogiela MR, Ogiela L, Ogiela U: Security and privacy in distributed information management. In: *2014 International conference on Intelligent Networking and Collaborative Systems (IEEE INCoS 2014), Salerno, Italy, September 10–12, 2014*, pp 73–78.

[14] Ogiela MR, Ogiela U, Ogiela L: Secure information sharing using personal biometric characteristics. In: Kim T, et al., editors: *4th International mega-conference on Future Generation Information Technology (FGIT 2012), Kangwondo, South Korea, December 16–19, 2012,* Berlin Heidelberg Springer-Verlag, Computer Applications for Bio-Technology, Multimedia, and Ubiquitous City, Communications in Computer and Information Science, vol. 353, 2012, pp 369–373.

[15] Ogiela MR, Ogiela L, Ogiela U: Biometric methods for advanced strategic data sharing protocols. In: *9th International conference on Innovative Mobile and Internet Services in ubiquitous computing (IMIS), Blumenau, Santa Catarina, Brazil 08–10 July 2015,* pp 179–183.

[16] Winston WL, Albright S: Practical management science, ed 5, USA, 2016, Cengage Learning.

[17] Zhang Q, Chen H, Shen Y, Ma S, Lu H: Optimization of virtual resource management for cloud applications to cope with traffic burst. *Future Gener Comput Syst* 58:42–55, 2016.

[18] Anderson DR, Sweeney DJ, Williams TA, Camm JD, Cochran JA: An introduction to management science: quantitative approaches to decision making, ed 14, USA, 2016, Cengage Learning.

[19] Fang D, Liu X, Romdhani I, Jamshidi P, Pahl C: An agility-oriented and fuzziness-embedded semantic model for collaborative cloud service search, retrieval and recommendation. *Future Gener Comput Syst* 56:11–26, 2016.

[20] TalebiFard P, Leung VCM: Context-aware mobility management in heterogeneous network environments. *J Wireless Mobile Networks Ubiquitous Comput Dependable Appl* 2(2):19–32, 2011.

[21] Ogiela L: Advanced techniques for knowledge management and access to strategic information. *Int J Inf Manage* 35:154–159, 2015.

[22] Banares JA, Altmann J, Vanmechelen K: Economics of computing services. *Future Gener Comput Syst* 55:401–402, 2016.

[23] Ning Y, Liu J, Yan L: Uncertain aggregate production planning. *Soft Comput* 17:617–624, 2012.

INTELLIGENT COGNITIVE INFORMATION SYSTEMS IN MANAGEMENT APPLICATIONS

6

Intelligent information systems designed for semantic description and interpretation tasks as well as processes of analyzing and understanding data have been developed as data understanding systems. In this context, they were described for various areas of data analysis. One of them is the management theory area. Solutions supporting data management processes are now generally recommended as capable of improving information management processes, limiting the cost, but primarily minimizing the risk of taking wrong decisions.

In data management the processes of analyzing data that is managed are particularly important. Obviously, the processes of managing data without its description or interpretation are very frequently executed alone, e.g., if the process is outsourced or if independent departments are established to execute these kinds of tasks. This is an example of an arrangement which does not always produce the appropriate solution. A new example of executing data management processes is a cognitive management process which includes the stage of analyzing and understanding data.

Systems which include solutions for the semantic understanding of data allow information, data, and situations that are to be managed to be assessed correctly. Understanding the essence of the managed entity allows the decision to be taken correctly, and also the data to be managed more efficiently by eliminating superfluous information. Cognitive management systems have been proposed to support the understanding of data in the form of ratios. This type of data is connected with the analysis of economic/financial ratios, which is aimed at the correct understanding of the standing of the enterprise and its future condition (situation).

Cognitive management systems have been split into different classes according to the type of data analyzed. However the purpose of all these classes is to support processes of managing strategic information. Cognitive data analysis systems which support management processes have been split into four main subclasses. This split stems from the interpretation of groups of financial ratios which influence the analyzed standing of the enterprise. This analysis can also be used to indicate the causes of the specific standing of the enterprise and to describe their meaning in this context.

Four main system classes have been distinguished in the group of systems supporting financial data management processes [1,2]:

- Cognitive UBMLRSS systems—Understanding Based Management Liquidity Ratios Support Systems—cognitive systems for analyzing enterprise liquidity ratios,
- Cognitive UBMARSS systems—Understanding Based Management Activity Ratios Support Systems—cognitive systems for analyzing turnover ratios,

- Cognitive UBMPRSS systems—Understanding Based Management Profitability Ratios Support Systems—cognitive systems for analyzing profitability ratios,
- Cognitive UBMFLRSS systems—Understanding Based Management Financial Leverage Ratios Support Systems—cognitive systems for analyzing financial leverage ratios (financial debt ratios).

The main job of cognitive management systems is to correctly interpret the current standing (taking into account the past condition and assessing the future condition) by understanding the determinants of this standing. To achieve this purpose, semantic data analysis algorithms are used in analysis and reasoning processes, as well as to support strategic decision-taking in management processes.

Semantic analysis processes are used to interpret varied sets of data that are subject to management processes. The semantic analysis executed in cognitive management systems allow the current standing of the enterprise to be determined, and also shows what decisions should be taken to improve the current standing or to maintain it—if the situation of enterprise is very good. This kind of analysis is conducted not only for a selected enterprise, but should also identify the impact of the external environment on its standing.

This is why systems for the semantic analysis of data used for analyzing and supporting enterprise management focus their action on [3]:

- analysis of the internal and external situation,
- predicting the future situation,
- improving decision-making processes,
- supporting strategic decision-making,
- supporting enterprise management processes,
- supporting enterprise management processes in the global aspects.

This situation is presented in Fig. 6.1.

The processes of analyzing and understanding data characterizing the situation of the enterprise are carried out by assessing various sets of data, of which the most important is information contained in ratios characterizing the entity [4–6].

Cognitive data analysis systems are used for a semantic analysis which consists in extracting semantic information from analyzed datasets and interpreting this information. Thus cognitive analysis processes ensure that data will be analyzed because of its significance. Linguistic formalisms in the form of definitions of formal grammars—sequential, tree, or graph—are used to describe the analyzed datasets. In the class of systems for managing financial information, linguistic formalisms in the form of sequential grammars have been adopted for formally describing the analyzed data [7–9].

The analysis of ratio data in cognitive management systems was proposed for the purpose of improving processes of strategic (financial) information management [10–12]. This improvement is achieved because linguistic formalisms are used in processes of analyzing financial data. This not only allows the analyzed values of financial ratios to be interpreted, but it also helps assess the situation of the enterprise and indicates the possible directions of its change if necessary or it shows that there is no need to implement any remedial action.

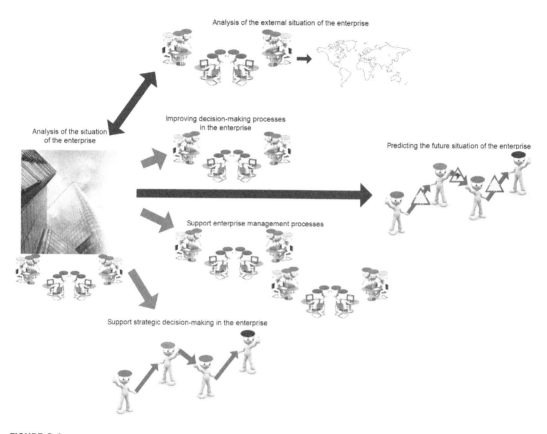

FIGURE 6.1

The enterprise management processes in the global aspects.

6.1 TYPES AND DIFFERENT WAYS OF INFORMATION FLOW IN COGNITIVE MANAGEMENT SYSTEMS

The flow of information plays a significant role in cognitive information management systems [6,13,14]. In this class of systems, the information flow depends on the type of structure in which the information is analyzed. From this point of view, the following structures are distinguished:

- hierarchical,
- layered, and
- mixed.

A hierarchical structure of the entity means that, in this type of structure, information flows between individual levels of the hierarchy, but also within specific levels. The first case is an example of information flowing between levels of the hierarchy and the second case represents a flow characteristic for a layered structure.

In hierarchical structures, information may flow (Fig. 6.2):

- between various levels of the hierarchy,
- within a specific level of the hierarchy,
- between a selected level of the hierarchy and another hierarchical level.

The second type of structures is layered ones. In this kind of structures, information most frequently flows within a given layer, but there can also be flows between different layers.

In layered structures, information may flow (Fig. 6.3):

- between different layers,
- within a given layers,
- between the selected layer and another one.

Both in hierarchical and in layered structures, flows are possible between the different rungs of the structure. This is an example of a flow characteristic for mixed structures. Within these structures, information flows (Fig. 6.4):

- between different layers,
- between various levels of the hierarchy,
- within a given layer,
- within a specific level of the hierarchy,
- between the selected layer and another one,
- between a selected level of the hierarchy and another hierarchical level,
- between selected layers and selected levels of the hierarchy.

Regardless of the information flow type, every piece of information is subject to analysis and understanding in cognitive management systems. The type of structure in which the analysis processes take place affects the rate of information flow and how this information is secured from disclosure to unauthorized persons. The execution of semantic data analysis processes is not directly dependent on the type of structure in which these processes are carried out.

6.2 CLASSIFICATION OF INTELLIGENT COGNITIVE SYSTEMS IN MANAGEMENT APPLICATIONS

Cognitive management systems are dedicated to the semantic analysis of economic/financial ratios and supplement simple information analysis. This way, these systems play the role of supporting the financial/strategic analysis of the entity (enterprise, organization, etc.). The main task of cognitive management systems is to conduct the financial analysis of a company using aspects of cognitive data analysis. This class of systems can be used for the semantic analysis of data carried out by understanding the sense (meaning) of the analyzed groups of ratios, in particular financial or macroeconomic.

Any group of ratios can be used for cognitive analysis aimed at understanding the semantic information contained in these sets.

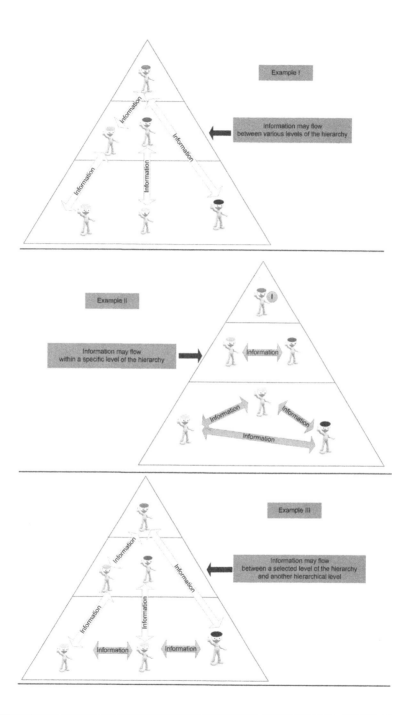

FIGURE 6.2

Information flow in a hierarchical structure.

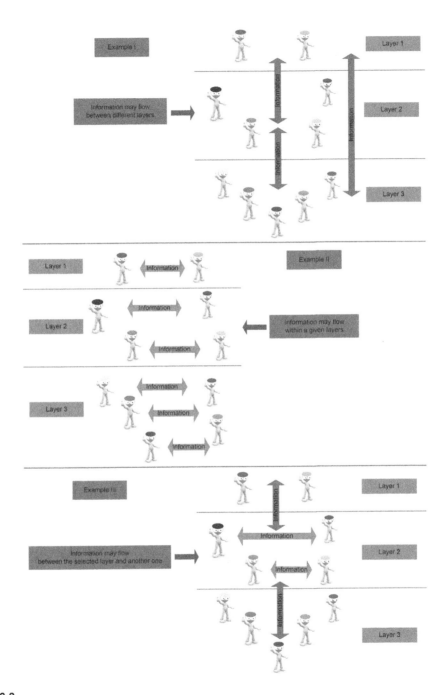

FIGURE 6.3

Information flow in a layered structure.

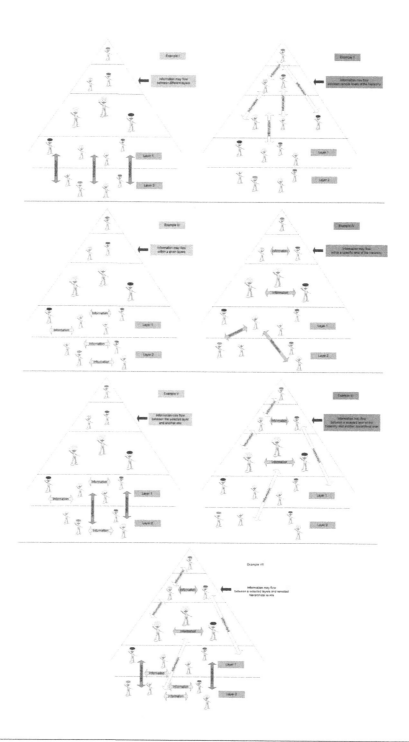

FIGURE 6.4

Information flow in a mixed structure.

Systems that support the process of managing financial data have been divided into the following four classes [15]:

- Cognitive UBMLRSS—Understanding Based Management Liquidity Ratios Support Systems— systems for analyzing enterprise liquidity ratios, which reason about the amount and the adequacy of the working capital of the company as well as about the company's current operations.
- Cognitive UBMARSS—Understanding Based Management Activity Ratios Support Systems— systems for analyzing turnover ratios, which reason about how fast assets rotate and how productive they are.
- Cognitive UBMPRSS—Understanding Based Management Profitability Ratios Support Systems— cognitive systems for analyzing profitability ratios, which reason about the financial efficiency of the business operations of a given unit based on the relationship between financial results, the sales of goods and services, and the cost of sales.
- Cognitive UBMFLRSS—Understanding Based Management Financial Leverage Ratios Support Systems—systems for analyzing financial leverage ratios (financial debt ratios), which reason about the sources financing the company's assets and the proportion of external capital by analyzing short-term and long-term liabilities, they also reason about the effectiveness of expenditure and the interest paid.

The classification of cognitive financial systems is shown in Fig. 6.5.

Fig. 6.5 shows the main groups of cognitive management systems and selected types of ratios in each subclass of cognitive systems. Within every group of financial ratios, many ratios used to analyze the standing of an enterprise are distinguished.

The first group of ratios are those describing the financial liquidity of the enterprise. The liquidity of an enterprise is understood as its ability to pay its current liabilities to, e.g., employees, suppliers,

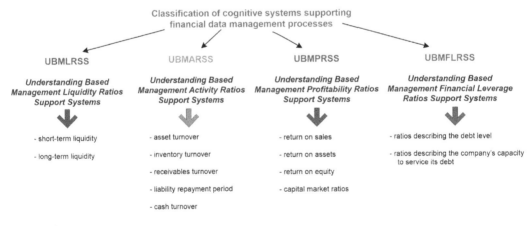

FIGURE 6.5

Classification of cognitive systems supporting management processes.

Source: Own development by Ogiela L, Ogiela MR: Efficiency of cognitive information systems supporting enterprise management tasks. In: 9th International conference on Innovative Mobile and Internet Services in ubiquitous computing (IMIS-2015), Blumenau, Santa Catarina, Brazil, 08–10 July 2015, pp 166–170 [16].

or banks, at maturity. This ability is determined by both the standing of the enterprise and the external situation independent outside its control.

The following ratios are distinguished in the group of ratios measuring liquidity:

- current ratio,
- quick ratio,
- cash ratio,
- mature payables ratio,
- cash flow indicator,
- cash flow coverage.

Within the group of ratios describing the cash flow of the enterprise, ratios of the cash flow to the following values are distinguished:

- sales,
- operating profit,
- assets,
- fixed assets,
- working capital.

Within the group of ratios defining cash flow coverage, the following indicators of cash flow coverage are distinguished:

- operating cash for paying total liabilities,
- operating cash for paying current liabilities,
- operating cash for paying long-term liabilities,
- general operating cash flow coverage,
- operating cash flow for fixed asset purchases.

Within the group of ratios describing the liquidity of an enterprise, the following indicators were adopted for the semantic analysis of ratios:

- the value of the current ratio,
- the value of the quick ratio,
- the value of the cash ratio,
- the value of the treasury ratio,
- the value of the mature payables ratio.

The next group of ratios are those describing the turnover cycles within the enterprise. The turnover is understood as the efficiency of the enterprise, i.e., the ability to make optimal use of the resources held by the enterprise in specific external conditions. Consequently, the turnover denotes the ability of the assets to generate revenues.

The following ratios are distinguished in the group of turnover indicators:

- asset turnover,
- fixed asset turnover,
- working asset turnover,
- liquid asset turnover.

Within the group of indicators describing the turnover cycles of an enterprise, the following were adopted for the semantic analysis of indicator data:

- the total asset turnover,
- the working asset turnover,
- the liquid asset turnover.

The next group of ratios are those describing the profitability (rate of return) of the enterprise. The profitability of the enterprise is understood as its ability to generate revenue from its operations, which revenue exceeds the operating cost of the enterprise. Profitability indicators measure the effectiveness of the entity's activities in the given (analyzed) period of time. Profitability ratios are very frequently used to assess the business of the company from the perspective of its ability to generate profit from the means that it uses. These ratios are employed to measure the degree to which the company has achieved its strategic goal of raising its value by boosting profitability.

The following ratios are distinguished in the group of profitability/rate of return indicators:

- return on sales,
- operating profitability of sales,
- profitability of business operations,
- return on gross sales,
- return on net sales,
- net profitability,
- cost level,
- return on assets,
- return on gross assets,
- return on net assets,
- return on gross assets including interest,
- return on fixed assets,
- return on working assets,
- return on clear assets,
- return on equity,
- equity market indicators.

Within the group of indicators measuring the profitability of an enterprise, the following were adopted for the semantic analysis of indicator data:

- the return on net assets,
- the return on gross assets,
- the return on gross assets including interest,
- the return on fixed assets,
- the return on working assets,
- the return on clear assets.

The last group of ratios are those describing the debt of the enterprise. Enterprise debt applies to a situation in which the enterprise uses any form of financial support and not exclusively its own capital. Hence it describes every situation in which the enterprise uses outside capital, which leads to the enterprise being in debt.

The assessment of the enterprise debt situation is aimed at determining the extent to which the enterprise finances itself with its own funds and to which it is financed with external funds. If the operations of the entity are financed with external funds, it is possible to assess the proportion of own equity to external capital in the entire financing of the enterprise. The most important element in assessing the debt situation is to determine the impact of external capital on enterprise operations and the degree to which the financial independence of the enterprise is at risk. This type of assessment leads to calculating the costs of using external capital and the cost-effectiveness of this solution.

The analysis of the value of debt ratios can concern debt level indicators and the ability of the enterprise to service this debt. The following ratios are distinguished in the group of ratios identifying the debt level:

- total debt ratio,
- long-term debt,
- debt to equity,
- long-term debt to equity,
- liability structure,
- long-term liability coverage with net fixed assets,
- interest coverage.

The following ratios are distinguished in the group of ratios measuring the ability of the enterprise to service its debt:

- debt service coverage,
- interest coverage,
- debt service coverage with the cash surplus.

Semantic data analysis systems are used to assess the current situation of the enterprise based on the semantic interpretation of a selected group of ratio data.

These classes of cognitive management systems may analyze [3]:

- the economic situation of enterprise,
- the surroundings of enterprise,
- the situation and condition of:
  - customers,
  - providers,
  - others companies,
- and the influence of the environment of the company.

In cognitive systems for the semantic analysis of data dedicated to understanding debt ratios, it is possible to determine:

- the degree to which enterprise operations are financed with its own funds,
- the degree to which enterprise operations are financed with external funds—the enterprise's debt,
- the proportion of own capital to external capital in corporate finance,
- the debt situation—by determining the impact of external capital on enterprise operations and the degree to which the financial independence of the enterprise is at risk,
- the costs and profitability of using external capital for enterprise operations.

Within the group of indicators measuring the financial leverage of an enterprise, the following were adopted for the semantic analysis of indicator data:

- the total debt ratio,
- the long-term debt ratio,
- the debt service coverage ratio,
- the value of the interest coverage ratio.

Based on the groups of indicators selected and adopted for the analysis, cognitive semantic analysis systems were proposed that are based on analyzing the value of selected groups of ratios characteristic for the operations of enterprises.

Semantic analysis is especially important for [1,2,17,18]:

- description of the present situation of enterprise,
- supporting the enterprise management processes,
- understanding of the current state of company,
- understanding of the reasons of the current state of the company,
- description of the future situation of enterprise.

The process of data mining in computer-aided enterprises management systems is shown in Fig. 6.6.

Data acquisition processes refer to collecting significant information about the standing of the analyzed entity. In the case of cognitive management systems, this information is found in sets of economic/financial ratios which are subjected to semantic data analysis processes. The information which forms the basis of these processes allows the standing of the entity (enterprise, organization, etc.) to be understood more fully, and also the processes of managing the analyzed data to be improved. Supplementing decision-making processes with the stage of semantic reasoning helps indicate groups of data which are of major importance for the correct operation of the enterprise and restrict (or eliminate) the influence of other factors.

6.3 INTERPRETATION AND DATA ANALYSIS PROCESSES IN COGNITIVE MANAGEMENT SYSTEM

The cognitive management systems have been proposed to perform semantic analysis of financial data and management processes. The semantic analysis of financial data allows to understand the company's situation. The cognitive management systems were divided into the different subclasses. In cognitive management systems the following classes were developed:

In UBMLRSS systems the following subclasses were developed [1,6,18,19]:

- UBMLRSS-$G_{(cu-q)}$—for analyzing ratio values:
  - v_{cu}—denotes the value of the current ratio,
  - v_q—denotes the value of the quick ratio,
- UBMLRSS-$G_{(cu-q-ca)}$—for analyzing ratio values:
  - v_{cu}—denotes the value of the current ratio,
  - v_q—denotes the value of the quick ratio,
  - v_{ca}—denotes the value of the cash ratio,

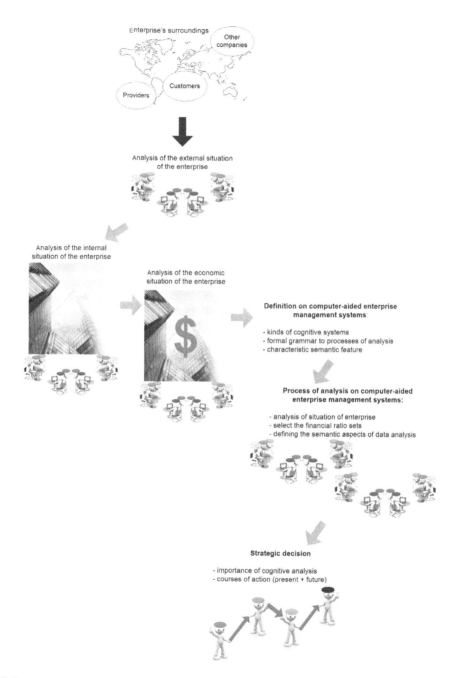

FIGURE 6.6

The process of data mining in computer-aided cognitive management systems.

- UBMLRSS-$G_{(cu\text{-}q\text{-}mp)}$—for analyzing ratio values:
  - v_{cu}—denotes the value of the current ratio,
  - v_q—denotes the value of the quick ratio,
  - v_{mp}—denotes the value of the mature payables ratio,
- UBMLRSS-$G_{(cu\text{-}ca\text{-}mp)}$—for analyzing ratio values:
  - v_{cu}—denotes the value of the current ratio,
  - v_{ca}—denotes the value of the cash ratio,
  - v_{mp}—denotes the value of the mature payables ratio,
- UBMLRSS-$G_{(q\text{-}ca\text{-}mp)}$—for analyzing ratio values:
  - v_q—denotes the value of the quick ratio,
  - v_{ca}—denotes the value of the cash ratio,
  - v_{mp}—denotes the value of the mature payables ratio,
- UBMLRSS-$G_{(cu\text{-}q\text{-}ca\text{-}tr)}$—for analyzing ratio values:
  - v_{cu}—denotes the value of the current ratio,
  - v_q—denotes the value of the quick ratio,
  - v_{ca}—denotes the value of the cash ratio,
  - v_{tr}—denotes the value of the treasury ratio.

In UBMARSS systems the following subclasses were developed [14]:

- UBMARSS-$G_{(ta\text{-}la)}$—for analyzing turnover indicators:
  - v_{ta}—denotes the total asset turnover,
  - v_{la}—denotes the liquid asset turnover,
- UBMARSS-$G_{(ta\text{-}wa)}$—for analyzing turnover indicators:
  - v_{ta}—denotes the total asset turnover,
  - v_{wa}—denotes the working asset turnover,
- UBMARSS-$G_{(ta\text{-}wa\text{-}la)}$—for analyzing turnover indicators:
  - v_{ta}—denotes the total asset turnover,
  - v_{wa}—denotes the working asset turnover,
  - v_{la}—denotes the liquid asset turnover.

In UBMPRSS systems the following subclasses were proposed [8]:

- UBMPRSS-$G_{(rna\text{-}rga\text{-}rgi)}$—for analyzing values:
  - v_{rna}—denotes the return on net assets,
  - v_{rga}—denotes the return on gross assets,
  - v_{rgi}—denotes the return on gross assets including interest,
- UBMPRSS-$G_{(rfa\text{-}rwa\text{-}rca)}$—for analyzing values:
  - v_{rfa}—denotes the return on fixed assets,
  - v_{rwa}—denotes the return on working assets,
  - v_{rca}—denotes the return on clear assets.

In UBMFLRSS systems the following subclasses were proposed [3]:

- UBMFLRSS-$G_{(td\text{-}ld)}$—for analyzing the debt value:
  - v_{td}—denotes the total debt ratio,
  - v_{ld}—denotes the long-term debt ratio,

- UBMFLRSS-$G_{(td\text{-}ls)}$—for analyzing the debt value:
  - v_{td}—denotes the total debt ratio,
  - v_{ls}—denotes the value of the liability structure ratio,
- UBMFLRSS-$G_{(dsc\text{-}ic)}$—for analyzing the debt value:
  - v_{dsc}—denotes the debt service coverage ratio,
  - v_{ic}—denotes the value of the interest coverage ratio.

In addition the cognitive analysis was conducted to merge the above selected subclasses of cognitive management systems. A cognitive analysis dedicated to cognitive financial management systems was proposed for particular classes:

- UBMLRSS-UBMPRSS-$G_{(mp\text{-}irr)}$—for analyzing values:
  - v_{mp}—denotes the value of the mature payables ratio,
  - v_{irr}—denotes the value of the internal rate of return,
- UBMLRSS-UBMPRSS-$G_{(q\text{-}irr)}$—for analyzing values:
  - v_q—denotes the value of the quick ratio,
  - v_{irr}—denotes the value of the internal rate of return,
- UBMLRSS-UBMPRSS-$G_{(mp\text{-}q\text{-}irr)}$—for analyzing values:
  - v_{mp}—denotes the value of the mature payables ratio,
  - v_q—denotes the value of the quick ratio,
  - v_{irr}—denotes the value of the internal rate of return,
- UBMLRSS-UBMPRSS-$G_{(cu\text{-}irr)}$—for analyzing values:
  - v_{cu}—denotes the value of the current ratio,
  - v_{irr}—denotes the value of the internal rate of return,
- UBMLRSS-UBMPRSS-$G_{(cu\text{-}q\text{-}irr)}$—for analyzing values:
  - v_{cu}—denotes the value of the current ratio,
  - v_q—denotes the value of the quick ratio,
  - v_{irr}—denotes the value of the internal rate of return,
- UBMLRSS-UBMPRSS-$G_{(ca\text{-}irr)}$—for analyzing values:
  - v_{ca}—denotes the value of the cash ratio,
  - v_{irr}—denotes the value of the internal rate of return,
- UBMLRSS-UBMPRSS-$G_{(ca\text{-}q\text{-}irr)}$—for analyzing values:
  - v_{ca}—denotes the value of the cash ratio,
  - v_q—denotes the value of the quick ratio,
  - v_{irr}—denotes the value of the internal rate of return,
- UBMARSS-UBMPRSS-$G_{(ta\text{-}irr)}$—for analyzing values:
  - v_{ta}—denotes the value of the total asset turnover indicator,
  - v_{irr}—denotes the value of the internal rate of return,
- UBMARSS-UBMPRSS-$G_{(wa\text{-}irr)}$—for analyzing values:
  - v_{wa}—denotes the value of the working asset turnover indicator,
  - v_{irr}—denotes the value of the internal rate of return,
- UBMARSS-UBMPRSS-$G_{(ta\text{-}wa\text{-}irr)}$—for analyzing values:
  - v_{ta}—denotes the value of the total asset turnover indicator,
  - v_{wa}—denotes the value of the working asset turnover indicator,
  - v_{irr}—denotes the value of the internal rate of return.

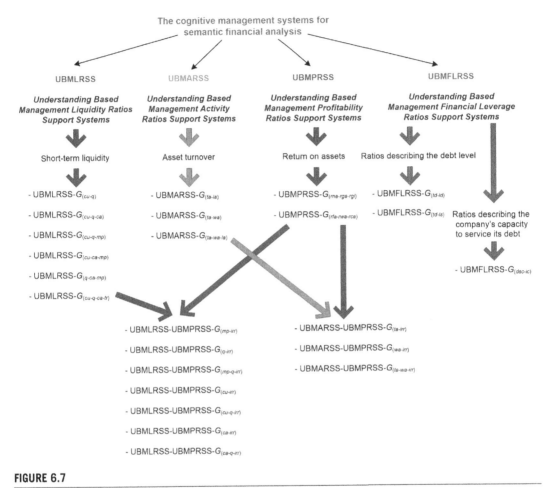

FIGURE 6.7

Classification of cognitive management systems dedicated to semantic financial analysis.

Cognitive systems, supported management processes, may analyzed combinations of different kinds of turnover ratios, financial leverage ratios, profitability ratios, and liquidity ratios. All proposed classes of cognitive management systems are shown in Fig. 6.7.

The processes of interpreting and analyzing various types of financial data are executed in cognitive management systems by assessing indicator parameters characteristic for the given group of ratios. To analyze and interpret the data, certain numerical intervals are adopted, which are characteristic of the specific standing of the entity and the behaviors resulting from it—steps that need to be taken. The proper definition of the correct presentation of data in the numerical, interval form, is necessary to understand the situation of the analyzed entity (e.g., an enterprise). These definitions are made at the stage of building the semantic data analysis algorithms in the form of formal grammars. A sequential form of the grammar makes it possible to account for all cases characteristic for the assessed situations.

The analysis process is executed by using linguistic formalisms to describe the indicator parameters adopted for a given entity. The number of parameters analyzed depends on the quantity of data acquired. The interpretation process consists in assessing the similarity of the analyzed data to models adopted when defining the cognitive management system as the best reflection of the optimal standing of an entity. Determining the level of similarity may impact the analysis of a given situation, but one should remember that the system can be taught new solutions that are more adequate for the analyzed data and which describe the condition of the analyzed entities.

System supporting management processes are designed for analyzing and assessing the standing of the entity analyzed by the system and for reasoning about its condition based on a semantic analysis of data (understanding the current standing).

6.4 USE CASES OF COGNITIVE INFORMATION SYSTEMS IN MANAGEMENT APPLICATIONS

Examples of cognitive systems supporting management processes have been developed by analyzing the groups of ratios presented in Section 6.3. There are many examples of the use of semantic analyses for the purpose of understanding a given situation. They will be presented below as examples of using the semantic analysis of financial data in the process of its understanding.

In UBMLRSS systems the following subclasses were proposed:

- UBMLRSS-$G_{(cu-q)}$—for analyzing ratio values:
  - v_{cu}—denotes the value of the current ratio,
  - v_q—denotes the value of the quick ratio,

$$G_{(cu-q)} = \left(V_{N(cu-q)}, V_{T(cu-q)}, P_{(cu-q)}, S_{(cu-q)}\right) \tag{6.1}$$

where

$V_{N(cu-q)}$ = {LIQUIDITY1, EXCESS_LIQUIDITY1, OPTIMAL_LIQUIDITY1, SOLVENCY_
    PROBLEMS1}—the set of non-terminal symbols,
$V_{T(cu-q)}$ = {a, b, c, d, e}—the set of terminal symbols,
    where a ∈ [0; 1), b ∈ [1; 1,2], c ∈ (1,2; 1,5), d ∈ [1,5; 2], e ∈ (2; + ∞)
$S_{(cu-q)}$ ∈ $V_{N(cu-q)}$,
$S_{(cu-q)}$ = LIQUIDITY1,
$P_{(cu-q)}$—set of productions:
1. LIQUIDITY1 → EXCESS_LIQUIDITY1 I OPTIMAL_LIQUIDITY1 I
   SOLVENCY_PROBLEMS1
2. **EXCESS_LIQUIDITY1** → DB I DC I DD
3. **OPTIMAL_LIQUIDITY1** → CB I CC I CD I DA I DE I EB I EC I ED
4. **SOLVENCY_PROBLEMS1** → AA I AB I AC I AD I AE I BA I BB I BC I BD I BE I CA I
   CE I EA I EE
5. A → a
6. B → b

      7. C → c
      8. D → d
      9. E → e

- UBMLRSS-$G_{(cu\text{-}q\text{-}ca)}$—for analyzing ratio values:
  - v_{cu}—denotes the value of the current ratio,
  - v_q—denotes the value of the quick ratio,
  - v_{ca}—denotes the value of the cash ratio,

$$G_{(cu-q-ca)} = \left(V_{N(cu-q-ca)}, V_{T(cu-q-ca)}, P_{(cu-q-ca)}, S_{(cu-q-ca)} \right) \tag{6.2}$$

where

$V_{N(cu\text{-}q\text{-}ca)}$ = {LIQUIDITY2, EXCESS_LIQUIDITY2, OPTIMAL_LIQUIDITY2, SOLVENCY_
        PROBLEMS2}—the set of non-terminal symbols,
$V_{T(cu\text{-}q\text{-}ca)}$ = {a, b, c, d, e}—the set of terminal symbols,
        where a ∈ [0; 1), b ∈ [1; 1,2], c ∈ (1,2; 1,5), d ∈ [1,5; 2], e ∈ (2; + ∞)
$S_{(cu\text{-}q\text{-}ca)}$ ∈ $V_{N(cu\text{-}q\text{-}ca)}$,
$S_{(cu\text{-}q\text{-}ca)}$ = LIQUIDITY2,
$P_{(cu\text{-}q\text{-}ca)}$—set of productions:
     1. LIQUIDITY2 → EXCESS_LIQUIDITY2 | OPTIMAL_LIQUIDITY2 |
        SOLVENCY_PROBLEMS2
     2. EXCESS_LIQUIDITY2 → EEE | EDE | EED
     3. OPTIMAL_LIQUIDITY2 → DCA | DCB | DBB | DBC | DBA | CBA | CCA | CBD
     4. SOLVENCY_PROBLEMS2 → DEE | AAA | ABA | AAB | ABB | BAB | BBA | ABC |
        BAC | ACB | BCA | AAC | ACA | CAA | AAD | ADA | DAA | AAE | AEA | EAA | ACD |
        ADC | ABD | ADB | DAB | ABE | AEB | BAA | BAD | BAE | BEA | EAB | EBA | CAB |
        ACC | CAC | BCC | CAD | CDA | CAE | CEA | ACE | ADE | AED | DAE | DEA | EAD |
        EDA | BBB | CCC | DDD | BBC | CBB | BDA | BCB | BBD | BDB | BBE | BEB | EBB |
        CCD | CDC | DCC | CCE | CEC | ECC | DDE | DED | EDD | BCD | BDC | CDB | BCE |
        BEC | ECB | EBC | CBE | CEB | CDE | CED | EDC | ECD | DEC | DCE | EEA | EAE |
        AEE | EEB | EBE | BEE | CEE | ECE | EEC | DDA | DAD | ADD | BDD | DBD | DDB |
        DDC | CDD | DCD | BDE | BED | CBC | CCB | DAC | DBE | EAC | EBD | ECA | EDB |
        AEC | DEB
     5. A → a
     6. B → b
     7. C → c
     8. D → d
     9. E → e

- UBMLRSS $G_{(cu\text{-}q\text{-}mp)}$—for analyzing ratio values:
  - v_{cu}—denotes the value of the current ratio,
  - v_q—denotes the value of the quick ratio,
  - v_{mp}—denotes the value of the mature payables ratio,

$$G_{(cu-q-mp)} = \left(V_{N(cu-q-mp)}, V_{T(cu-q-mp)}, P_{(cu-q-mp)}, S_{(cu-q-mp)} \right) \tag{6.3}$$

where

$V_{N(cu-q-mp)}$ = {LIQUIDITY3, EXCESS_LIQUIDITY3, OPTIMAL_LIQUIDITY3, SOLVENCY_
      PROBLEMS3}—the set of non-terminal symbols,

$V_{T(cu-q-mp)}$ = {a, b, c, d, e}—the set of terminal symbols,
      where a ∈ [0; 1), b ∈ [1; 1,2], c ∈ (1,2; 1,5), d ∈ [1,5; 2], e ∈ (2; + ∞),

$S_{(cu-q-mp)}$ ∈ $V_{N(cu-q-mp)}$,

$S_{(cu-q-mp)}$ = LIQUIDITY3,

$P_{(cu-q-mp)}$—set of productions:
1. **LIQUIDITY3** → EXCESS_LIQUIDITY3 I OPTIMAL_LIQUIDITY3 I
   SOLVENCY_PROBLEMS3
2. **EXCESS_LIQUIDITY3** → EEE I EDE I EED
3. **OPTIMAL_LIQUIDITY3**→ DCA I DCB I DCC I DCD I DCE I DBB I DBC I DBA I DBD
   I DBE I CBA I CBB I CBC I CBD I CBE I CCA I CCB I CCC I CCD I CCE
4. **SOLVENCY_PROBLEMS3** → DEE I AAA I ABA I AAB I ABB I BAB I BBA I ABC I
   BAC I ACB I BCA I AAC I ACA I CAA I AAD I ADA I DAA I AAE I AEA I EAA I ACD I
   ADC I ABD I ADB I DAB I ABE I AEB I BAA I BAD I BAE I BEA I EAB I EBA I CAB I
   ACC I CAC I BCC I CAD I CDA I CAE I CEA I ACE I ADE I AED I DAE I DEA I EAD I
   EDA I BBB I DDD I BBC I BDA I BCB I BBD I BDB I BBE I BEB I EBB I CDC I CEC I
   ECC I DDE I DED I EDD I BCD I BDC I CDB I BCE I BEC I ECB I EBC I CEB I CDE I
   CED I EDC I ECD I DEC I EEA I EAE I AEE I EEB I EBE I BEE I CEE I ECE I EEC I DDA
   I DAD I ADD I BDD I DDB I DDC I CDD I BDE I BED I DAC I EAC I EBD I ECA I EDB I
   AEC I DEB
5. **A** → a
6. **B** → b
7. **C** → c
8. **D** → d
9. **E** → e

- UBMLRSS $G_{(cu-ca-mp)}$—for analyzing ratio values:
  - v_{cu}—denotes the value of the current ratio,
  - v_{ca}—denotes the value of the cash ratio,
  - v_{mp}—denotes the value of the mature payables ratio,

$$G_{(cu-ca-mp)} = \left(V_{N(cu-ca-mp)}, V_{T(cu-ca-mp)}, P_{(cu-ca-mp)}, S_{(cu-ca-mp)} \right) \tag{6.4}$$

where

$V_{N(cu-ca-mp)}$ = {LIQUIDITY4, EXCESS_LIQUIDITY4, OPTIMAL_LIQUIDITY4, SOLVENCY_
      PROBLEMS4}—the set of non-terminal symbols,

$V_{T(cu-ca-mp)}$ = {a, b, c, d, e}—the set of terminal symbols,
      where a ∈ [0; 1), b ∈ [1; 1,2], c ∈ (1,2; 1,5), d ∈ [1,5; 2], e ∈ (2; + ∞),

$S_{(cu-ca-mp)} \in V_{N(cu-ca-mp)}$,

$S_{(cu-ca-mp)} = \text{LIQUIDITY4}$,

$P_{(cu-ca-mp)}$—set of productions:

1. LIQUIDITY4 → EXCESS_LIQUIDITY4 I OPTIMAL_LIQUIDITY4 I SOLVENCY_PROBLEMS4
2. **EXCESS_LIQUIDITY4** → EEE I EDE I EED I EEC
3. **OPTIMAL_LIQUIDITY4**→ DCA I DCB I DCC I DCD I DCE I DBA I DBB I DBC I DBD I DBE I CBA I CBB I CBC I CBD I CBE I CCA I CCB I CCC I CCD I CCE
4. **SOLVENCY_PROBLEMS4** → DEE I AAA I ABA I AAB I ABB I BAB I BBA I ABC I BAC I ACB I BCA I AAC I ACA I CAA I AAD I ADA I DAA I AAE I AEA I EAA I ACD I ADC I ABD I ADB I DAB I ABE I AEB I BAA I BAD I BAE I BEA I EAB I EBA I CAB I ACC I CAC I BCC I CAD I CDA I CAE I CEA I ACE I ADE I AED I DAE I DEA I EAD I EDA I BBB I DDD I BBC I BDA I BCB I BBD I BDB I BBE I BEB I EBB I CDC I CEC I ECC I DDE I DED I EDD I BCD I BDC I CDB I BCE I BEC I ECB I EBC I CEB I CDE I CED I EDC I ECD I DEC I EEA I EAE I AEE I EEB I EBE I BEE I CEE I ECE I DDA I DAD I ADD I BDD I DDB I DDC I CDD I BDE I BED I DAC I EAC I EBD I ECA I EDB I AEC I DEB
5. A → a
6. B → b
7. C → c
8. D → d
9. E → e

- UBMLRSS $G_{(q-ca-mp)}$—for analyzing ratio values:
  - v_q—denotes the value of the quick ratio,
  - v_{ca}—denotes the value of the cash ratio,
  - v_{mp}—denotes the value of the mature payables ratio,

$$G_{(q-ca-mp)} = \left(V_{N(q-ca-mp)}, V_{T(q-ca-mp)}, P_{(q-ca-mp)}, S_{(q-ca-mp)} \right) \tag{6.5}$$

where

$V_{N(q-ca-mp)} = \{\text{LIQUIDITY5, EXCESS\_LIQUIDITY5, OPTIMAL\_LIQUIDITY5, SOLVENCY\_PROBLEMS5}\}$—the set of non-terminal symbols,

$V_{T(q-ca-mp)} = \{a, b, c, d, e\}$—the set of terminal symbols,
    where $a \in [0; 1)$, $b \in [1; 1,2]$, $c \in (1,2; 1,5)$, $d \in [1,5; 2]$, $e \in (2; +\infty)$,

$S_{(q-ca-mp)} \in V_{N(q-ca-mp)}$,

$S_{(q-ca-mp)} = \text{LIQUIDITY5}$,

$P_{(q-ca-mp)}$—set of productions:

1. LIQUIDITY5 → EXCESS_LIQUIDITY5 I OPTIMAL_LIQUIDITY5 I SOLVENCY_PROBLEMS5
2. **EXCESS_LIQUIDITY5** → EEE I EDE I EED I EEC I DDC I DDD I DDE I DED I DEE I EDD
3. **OPTIMAL_LIQUIDITY5** → DCA I DCB I DCC I DCD I DCE I DBA I DBB I DBC I DBD I DBE I CBA I CBB I CBC I CBD I CBE I CCA I CCB I CCC I CCD I CCE I BBA I

BBB I BBC I BBD I BBE I BCA I BCB I BCC I BCD I BCE I BDA I BDB I BDC I BDD I BDE I BEA I BEB I BEC I BED I BEE

4. **SOLVENCY_PROBLEMS5** → AAA I ABA I AAB I ABB I BAB I ABC I BAC I ACB I AAC I ACA I CAA I AAD I ADA I DAA I AAE I AEA I EAA I ACD I ADC I ABD I ADB I DAB I ABE I AEB I BAA I BAD I BAE I EAB I EBA I CAB I ACC I CAC I CAD I CDA I CAE I CEA I ACE I ADE I AED I DAE I DEA I EAD I EDA I EBB I CDC I CEC I ECC I CDB I ECB I EBC I CEB I CDE I CED I EDC I ECD I DEC I EEA I EAE I AEE I EEB I EBE I CEE I ECE I DDA I DAD I ADD I DDB I CDD I DAC I EAC I EBD I ECA I EDB I AEC I DEB

5. A → a
6. B → b
7. C → c
8. D → d
9. E → e

- UBMLRSS-G$_{(cu-q-ca-tr)}$—for analyzing ratio values:
  - v_{cu}—denotes the value of the current ratio,
  - v_q—denotes the value of the quick ratio,
  - v_{ca}—denotes the value of the cash ratio,
  - v_{tr}—denotes the value of the treasury ratio,

$$G_{(cu-q-ca-tr)} = \left(V_{N(cu-q-ca-tr)}, V_{T(cu-q-ca-tr)}, P_{(cu-q-ca-tr)}, S_{(cu-q-ca-tr)}\right) \quad (6.6)$$

where

$V_{N(cu-q-ca-tr)}$ = {LIQUIDITY6, EXCESS_LIQUIDITY6, OPTIMAL_LIQUIDITY6, SOLVENCY_PROBLEMS6}—the set of non-terminal symbols,

$V_{T(cu-q-ca-tr)}$ = {a, b, c, d, e}—the set of terminal symbols, where a ∈ [0; 1), b ∈ [1; 1,2], c ∈ (1,2; 1,5), d ∈ [1,5; 2], e ∈ (2; + ∞),

$S_{(cu-q-ca-tr)}$ ∈ $V_{N(cu-q-ca-tr)}$,

$S_{(cu-q-ca-tr)}$=LIQUIDITY6,

$P_{(cu-q-ca-tr)}$—set of productions:

1. LIQUIDITY6 → EXCESS_LIQUIDITY6 I OPTIMAL_LIQUIDITY6 I SOLVENCY_PROBLEMS6
2. **EXCESS_LIQUIDITY6** → EEEE I EDEE I EDED I EEDE I EEDD I EEED
3. **OPTIMAL_LIQUIDITY6** → DCAA I DCAB I DCAC I DCAD I DCAE I DCBA I DCBB I DCBC I DCBD I DCBE I DBBA I DBBB I DBBC I DBBD I DBBE I DBCA I DBCB I DBCC I DBCD I DBCE I DBAA I DBAB I DBAC I DBAD I DBAE I CBAA I CBAB I CBAC I CBAD I CBAE I CCAA I CCAB I CCAC I CCAD I CCAE I CBDA I CBDB I CBDC I CBDD I CBDE
4. **SOLVENCY_PROBLEMS6** → DEEA I DEEB I DEEC I DEED I DEEE I AAAA I AAAB I AAAC I AAAD I AAAE I ABAA I ABAB I ABAC I ABAD I ABAE I AABA I AABB I AABC I AABD I AABE I ABBA I ABBB I ABBC I ABBD I ABBE I BABA I BABB I BABC I BABD I BABE I BBAA I BBAB I BBAC I BBAD I BBAE I ABCA I ABCB I ABCC I ABCD I ABCE I BACA I BACB I BACC I BACD I BACE I ACBA I ACBB I ACBC

I ACBD I ACBE I BCAA I BCAB I BCAC I BCAD I BCAE I AACA I AACB I AACC I
AACD I AACE I ACAA I ACAB I ACAC I ACAD I ACAE I CAAA I CAAB I CAAC I
CAAD I CAAE I AADA I AADB I AADC I AADD I AADE I ADAA I ADAB I ADAC I
ADAD I ADAE I DAAA I DAAB I DAAC I DAAD I DAAE I AAEA I AAEB I AAEC I
AAED I AAEE I AEAA I AEAB I AEAC I AEAD I AEAE I EAAA I EAAB I EAAC I
EAAD I EAAE I ACDA I ACDB I ACDC I ACDD I ACDE I ADCA I ADCB I ADCC I
ADCD I ADCE I ABDA I ABDB I ABDC I ABDD I ABDE I ADBA I ADBB I ADBC I
ADBD I ADBE I DABA I DABB I DABC I DABD I DABE I ABEA I ABEB I ABEC I
ABED I ABEE I AEBA I AEBB I AEBC I AEBD I AEBE I BAAA I BAAB I BAAC I BAAD
I BAAE I BADA I BADB I BADC I BADD I BADE I BAEA I BEAB I BAEC I BAED I
BAEE I BEAA I BAEB I BEAC I BEAD I BEAE I EABA I EABB I EABC I EABD I EABE
I EBAA I EBAB I EBAC I EBAD I EBAE I CABA I CABB I CABC I CABD I CABE I
ACCA I ACCB I ACCC I ACCD I ACCE I CACA I CACB I CACC I CACD I CACE I BCCA
I BCCB I BCCC I BCCD I BCCE I CADA I CADB I CADC I CADD I CADE I CDAA
I CDAB I CDAC I CDAD I CDAE I CAEA I CAEB I CAEC I CAED I CAEE I CEAA I
CEAB I CEAC I CEAD I CEAE I ACEA I ACEB I ACEC I ACED I ACEE I ADEA I ADEB I
ADEC I ADED I ADEE I AEDA I AEDB I AEDC I AEDD I AEDE I DAEA I DAEB I DAEC
I DAED I DAEE I DEAA I DEAB I DEAC I DEAD I DEAE I EADA I EADB I EADC I
EADD I EADE I EDAA I EDAB I EDAC I EDAD I EDAE I BBBA I BBBB I BBBC I BBBD
I BBBE I CCCA I CCCB I CCCC I CCCD I CCCE I CDCD I DCDC I DCEB I DDDA
I DDDB I DDDC I DDDD I DDDE I BBCA I BBCB I BBCC I BBCD I BBCE I CBBA
I CBBB I CBBC I CBBD I CBBE I BDAA I BDAB I BDAC I BDAD I BDAE I BCBA
I BCBB I BCBC I BCBD I BCBE I BBDA I BBDB I BBDC I BBDD I BBDE I BDBA I
BDBB I BDBC I BDBD I BDBE I BBEA I BBEB I BBEC I BBED I BBEE I BEBA I BEBB
I BEBC I BEBD I BEBE I EBBA I EBBB I EBBC I EBBD I EBBE I CCDA I CCDB I CCDC
I CCDD I CCDE I CDCA I CDCB I CDCC I CDCE I DCCA I DCCB I DCCC I DCCD I
DCCE I CCEA I CCEB I CCEC I CCED I CCEE I CECA I CECB I CECC I CECD I CECE I
ECCA I ECCB I ECCC I ECCD I ECCE I DDEA I DDEB I DDEC I DDED I DDEE I DEDA
I DEDB I DEDC I DEDD I DEDE I EDDA I EDDB I EDDC I EDDD I EDDE I BCDA I
BCDB I BCDC I BCDD I BCDE I BDCA I BDCB I BDCC I BDCD I BDCE I CDBA I
CDBB I CDBC I CDBD I CDBE I BCEA I BCEB I BCEC I BCED I BCEE I BECA I BECB
I BECC I BECD I BECE I ECBA I ECBB I ECBC I ECBD I ECBE I EBCA I EBCB I EBCC
I EBCD I EBCE I CBEA I CBEB I CBEC I CBED I CBEE I CEBA I CEBB I CEBC I CEBD
I CEBE I CDEA I CDEB I CDEC I CDED I CDEE I CEDA I CEDB I CEDC I CEDD I
CEDE I EDCA I EDCB I EDCC I EDCD I EDCE I ECDA I ECDB I ECDC I ECDD I ECDE
I DECA I DECB I DECC I DECD I DECE I DCEA I DCEC I DCED I DCEE I EEAA I
EEAB I EEAC I EEAD I EEAE I EAEA I EAEB I EAEC I EAED I EAEE I AEEA I AEEB
I AEEC I AEED I AEEE I EEBA I EEBB I EEBC I EEBD I EEBE I EBEA I EBEB I EBEC
I EBED I EBEE I BEEA I BEEB I BEEC I BEED I BEEE I CEEA I CEEB I CEEC I CEED
I CEEE I ECEA I ECEB I ECEC I ECED I ECEE I EECA I EECB I EECC I EECD I EECE
I DDAA I DDAB I DDAC I DDAD I DDAE I DADA I DADB I DADC I DADD I DADE
I ADDA I ADDB I ADDC I ADDD I ADDE I BDDA I BDDB I BDDC I BDDD I BDDE
I DBDA I DBDB I DBDC I DBDD I DBDE I DDBA I DDBB I DDBC I DDBD I DDBE
I DDCA I DDCB I DDCC I DDCD I DDCE I CDDA I CDDB I CDDC I CDDD I CDDE

| DCDA | DCDB | DCDD | DCDE | BDEA | BDEB | BDEC | BDED | BDEE | BEDA |
BEDB | BEDC | BEDD | BEDE | CBCA | CBCB | CBCC | CBCD | CBCE | CCBA | CCBB
| CCBC | CCBD | CCBE | DACA | DACB | DACC | DACD | DACE | DBEA | DBEB |
DBEC | DBED | DBEE | EACA | EACB | EACC | EACD | EACE | EBDA | EBDB | EBDC
| EBDD | EBDE | ECAA | ECAB | ECAC | ECAD | ECAE | EDBA | EDBB | EDBC |
EDBD | EDBE | EDEA | EDEB | EDEC | EEDA | EEDB | EEDC | EEEA | EEEB | EEEC |
AECA | AECB | AECC | AECD | AECE | DEBA | DEBB | DEBC | DEBD | DEBE

  5. A → a
  6. B → b
  7. C → c
  8. D → d
  9. E → e

Presented examples of cognitive information systems, supported management processes, are combinations of two, three, or four different types of financial ratios.

The cognitive management systems allow to analyze the following cases:

- excess liquidity,
- optimal liquidity,
- solvency problems.

In UBMARSS systems were proposed the following subclasses:

- UBMARSS-$G_{(ta\text{-}la)}$—for analyzing turnover indicators:
  - v_{ta}—denotes the total asset turnover,
  - v_{la}—denotes the liquid asset turnover,

$$G_{(ta-la)} = \left(V_{N(ta-la)}, V_{T(ta-la)}, P_{(ta-la)}, S_{(ta-la)} \right) \tag{6.7}$$

where

$V_{N(ta\text{-}la)} = \{$ASSET_TURNOVER1, LOW_TURNOVER1, MEDIUM_TURNOVER1, HIGH_
        TURNOVER1$\}$—the set of non-terminal symbols,
$V_{T(ta\text{-}la)}$—denotes the set of terminal symbols:
$V_{T(ta\text{-}la)} = \{$a, b, c$\}$, where a ∈ [0; 1], b ∈ (1; 3], c ∈ (3; + ∞)
$S_{(ta\text{-}la)} \in V_{N(ta\text{-}la)}$, $S_{(ta\text{-}la)}$=ASSET_TURNOVER1
$P_{(ta\text{-}la)}$—denotes the set of productions:
  1. ASSET_TURNOVER1 → LOW_TURNOVER1 | MEDIUM_TURNOVER1 |
    HIGH_TURNOVER1
  2. LOW_TURNOVER1 → AA | AB | AC
  3. MEDIUM_TURNOVER1 → BA | BB | CA
  4. HIGH_TURNOVER1 → BC | CB | CC
  5. A → a
  6. B → b
  7. C → c.

- UBMARSS-$G_{(ta\text{-}wa)}$—for analyzing turnover indicators:
  - v_{ta}—denotes the total asset turnover,
  - v_{wa}—denotes the working asset turnover,

$$G_{(ta-wa)} = \left(V_{N(ta-wa)}, V_{T(ta-wa)}, P_{(ta-wa)}, S_{(ta-wa)} \right) \tag{6.8}$$

where

$V_{N(ta\text{-}wa)}$ = {ASSET_TURNOVER2, LOW_TURNOVER2, MEDIUM_TURNOVER2, HIGH_
 TURNOVER2}—the set of non-terminal symbols,
$V_{T(ta\text{-}wa)}$—denotes the set of terminal symbols:
$V_{T(ta\text{-}wa)}$ = {a, b, c}, where a $\in$ [0; 1], b $\in$ (1; 3], c $\in$ (3; + ∞)
$S_{(ta\text{-}wa)} \in V_{N(ta\text{-}wa)}$, $S_{(ta\text{-}wa)}$ = ASSET_TURNOVER2
$P_{(ta\text{-}wa)}$—denotes the set of productions:
  1. ASSET_TURNOVER2 → LOW_TURNOVER2 I MEDIUM_TURNOVER2 I
     HIGH_TURNOVER2
  2. **LOW_TURNOVER2** → AA I AB I AC
  3. **MEDIUM_TURNOVER2** → BA I BB I CA
  4. **HIGH_TURNOVER2** → BC I CB I CC
  5. A → a
  6. B → b
  7. C → c.

- UBMARSS-$G_{(ta\text{-}wa\text{-}la)}$—for analyzing turnover indicators:
  - v_{ta}—denotes the total asset turnover,
  - v_{wa}—denotes the working asset turnover,
  - v_{la}—denotes the liquid asset turnover,

$$G_{(ta-wa-la)} = \left(V_{N(ta-wa-la)}, V_{T(ta-wa-la)}, P_{(ta-wa-la)}, S_{(ta-wa-la)} \right) \tag{6.9}$$

where

$V_{N(ta\text{-}wa\text{-}la)}$ = {ASSET_TURNOVER3, LOW_TURNOVER3, MEDIUM_TURNOVER3, HIGH_
 TURNOVER3}—the set of non-terminal symbols,
$V_{T(ta\text{-}wa\text{-}la)}$—denotes the set of terminal symbols:
$V_{T(ta\text{-}wa\text{-}la)}$ = {a, b, c}, where a $\in$ [0; 1], b $\in$ (1; 3], c $\in$ (3; + ∞)
$S_{(ta\text{-}wa\text{-}la)} \in V_{N(ta\text{-}wa\text{-}la)}$, $S_{(ta\text{-}wa\text{-}la)}$ = ASSET_TURNOVER3
$P_{(ta\text{-}wa\text{-}la)}$—denotes the set of productions:
  1. ASSET_TURNOVER3 → LOW_TURNOVER3 I MEDIUM_TURNOVER3 I
     HIGH_TURNOVER3
  2. **LOW_TURNOVER3** → AAA I ABA I ACA I AAB I AAC I BAA I CAA I ABB
  3. **MEDIUM_TURNOVER3** → BAB I BBB I BAC I CAB I CAC I ABC I ACB I ACC I BBA I
     BCA I CBA I CCA
  4. **HIGH_TURNOVER3** → BCB I CBB I BBC I CCC I CCB I BCC I CBC
  5. A → a
  6. B → b
  7. C → c.

Presented examples of cognitive information systems, supported management processes, are combinations of two or three different types of financial ratios.

The cognitive management systems allow to analyze the following cases:

- low turnover,
- medium turnover,
- high turnover.

In UBMPRSS systems were proposed the following subclasses:

- UBMPRSS-$G_{(rna\text{-}rga\text{-}rgi)}$—for analyzing values:
  - v_{rna}—denotes the return on net assets,
  - v_{rga}—denotes the return on gross assets,
  - v_{rgi}—denotes the return on gross assets including interest,

$$G_{(rna-rga-rgi)} = \left(V_{N(rna-rga-rgi)}, V_{T(rna-rga-rgi)}, P_{(rna-rga-rgi)}, S_{(rna-rga-rgi)}\right) \qquad (6.10)$$

where

$V_{N(rna\text{-}rga\text{-}rgi)}$ = {PROFITABILITY_1, HIGH_PROFITABILITY1, PROFITABILITY1, UNPROFITABILITY1}—the set of non-terminal symbols,
$V_{T(rna\text{-}rga\text{-}rgi)}$—denotes the set of terminal symbols:
$V_{T(rna\text{-}rga\text{-}rgi)}$ = {a, b, c}, where a $\in$ [- 1; 0), b $\in$ [0; 0,65), c $\in$ [0,65; 1]
$S_{(rna\text{-}rga\text{-}rgi)} \in V_{N(rna\text{-}rga\text{-}rgi)}$, $S_{(rna\text{-}rga\text{-}rgi)}$ = PROFITABILITY_1
$P_{(rna\text{-}rga\text{-}rgi)}$—denotes the set of productions:
  1. PROFITABILITY_1 → HIGH_PROFITABILITY1 I PROFITABILITY1 I UNPROFITABILITY1
  2. **HIGH_PROFITABILITY1** → CCC
  3. **PROFITABILITY1** → BBB I BBC I BCB I CBB I CBC I BCC I CCB
  4. **UNPROFITABILITY1** → AAA I ABA I AAB I ABC I ACB I BAA I BAC I BCA I BAB I ABB I BBA I AAC I ACA I CAA I CAB I CBA I ACC I CAC I CCA
  5. A → a
  6. B → b
  7. C → c.

- UBMPRSS-$G_{(rfa\text{-}rwa\text{-}rca)}$—for analyzing values:
  - v_{rfa}—denotes the return on fixed assets,
  - v_{rwa}—denotes the return on working assets,
  - v_{rca}—denotes the return on clear assets,

$$G_{(rfa-rwa-rca)} = \left(V_{N(rfa-rwa-rca)}, V_{T(rfa-rwa-rca)}, P_{(rfa-rwa-rca)}, S_{(rfa-rwa-rca)}\right) \qquad (6.11)$$

where

$V_{N(rfa\text{-}rwa\text{-}rca)}$ = {PROFITABILITY_2, HIGH_PROFITABILITY2, PROFITABILITY2, UNPROFITABILITY2}—the set of non-terminal symbols,
$V_{T(rfa\text{-}rwa\text{-}rca)}$—denotes the set of terminal symbols:

$V_{T(rfa\text{-}rwa\text{-}rca)} = \{a, b, c\}$, where $a \in [-1; 0)$, $b \in [0; 0,60)$, $c \in [0,60; 1]$

$S_{(rfa\text{-}rwa\text{-}rca)} \in V_{N(rfa\text{-}rwa\text{-}rca)}$, $S_{(rfa\text{-}rwa\text{-}rca)}$=PROFITABILITY_2

$P_{(rfa\text{-}rwa\text{-}rca)}$—denotes the set of productions:

1. PROFITABILITY_2 → HIGH_PROFITABILITY2 I PROFITABILITY2 I UNPROFITABILITY2
2. **HIGH_PROFITABILITY2** → CCC
3. **PROFITABILITY2** → BBB I BBC I BCB I CBB I CBC I BCC I CCB
4. **UNPROFITABILITY2** → AAA I ABA I AAB I ABC I ACB I BAA I BAC I BCA I BAB I ABB I BBA I AAC I ACA I CAA I CAB I CBA I ACC I CAC I CCA
5. A → a
6. B → b
7. C → c.

Presented examples of cognitive information systems, supported management processes, are combinations of three different types of financial ratios.

The cognitive management systems allow to analyze the following cases:

- high profitability,
- profitability (good),
- unprofitability.

In UBMFLRSS systems were proposed the following subclasses:

- UBMFLRSS-$G_{(td\text{-}ld)}$—for analyzing the debt value:
  - v_{td}—denotes the total debt ratio,
  - v_{ld}—denotes the long-term debt ratio,

$$G_{(td-ld)} = \left(V_{N(td-ld)}, V_{T(td-ld)}, P_{(td-ld)}, S_{(td-ld)}\right) \tag{6.12}$$

where

$V_{N(td\text{-}ld)} = \{DEBT1, HIGH\_DEBT1, OPTIMAL\_DEBT1, LOW\_DEBT1\}$—the set of non-terminal symbols,

$V_{T(td\text{-}ld)} = \{a, b, c\}$—the set of terminal symbols,
where $a \in [0; 0,57)$, $b \in [0,57; 0,67]$, $c \in (0,67; 1]$

$S_{(td\text{-}ld)} \in V_{N(td\text{-}ld)}$,

$S_{(td\text{-}ld)} = DEBT1$,

$P_{(td\text{-}ld)}$—denotes the set of productions:

1. DEBT1 →HIGH_DEBT1 I OPTIMAL_DEBT1 I LOW_DEBT1
2. **HIGH_DEBT1** → BC I CB I CC
3. **OPTIMAL_DEBT1** → BB
4. **LOW_DEBT1** → AA I AB I AC I CA I CB
5. A → a
6. B → b
7. C → c.

- UBMFLRSS-$G_{(td\text{-}ls)}$—for analyzing the debt value:
  - v_{td}—denotes the total debt ratio,
  - v_{ls}—denotes the value of the liability structure ratio,

$$G_{(td-ls)} = \left(V_{N(td-ls)}, V_{T(td-ls)}, P_{(td-ls)}, S_{(td-ls)}\right) \tag{6.13}$$

where

$V_{N(td\text{-}ls)}$ = {DEBT2, HIGH_DEBT2, OPTIMAL_DEBT2, LOW_DEBT2}—the set of non-terminal symbols,

$V_{T(td\text{-}ls)}$ = {a, b, c}—the set of terminal symbols,
      where a ∈ [0; 0,57), b ∈ [0,57; 0,67], c ∈ (0,67; 1]

$S_{(td\text{-}ls)}$ ∈ $V_{N(td\text{-}ls)}$,

$S_{(td\text{-}ls)}$ = DEBT2,

$P_{(td\text{-}ls)}$—set of productions:
  1. DEBT2 →HIGH_DEBT2 I OPTIMAL_DEBT2 I LOW_DEBT2
  2. **HIGH_DEBT2** → CC
  3. **OPTIMAL_DEBT2**→ BB I BC I CB
  4. **LOW_DEBT2** → AA I AB I AC I BA I CA
  5. A → a
  6. B → b
  7. C → c.

- UBMFLRSS-$G_{(dsc\text{-}ic)}$—for analyzing the debt value:
  - v_{dsc}—denotes the debt service coverage ratio,
  - v_{ic}—denotes the value of the interest coverage ratio,

$$G_{(dsc-ic)} = \left(V_{N(dsc-ic)}, V_{T(dsc-ic)}, P_{(dsc-ic)}, S_{(dsc-ic)}\right) \tag{6.14}$$

where

$V_{N(dsc\text{-}ic)}$ = {DEBT_SERVICE1, HIGH_DEBTSERVICE1, MEDIUM_DEBTSERVICE1, LOW_DEBTSERVICE1}—the set of non-terminal symbols,

$V_{T(dsc\text{-}ic)}$ = {a, b, c}—the set of terminal symbols,
      where a ∈ [0; 1), b ∈ [1; 1,5], c ∈ (1,5; 2,5]

$S_{(dsc\text{-}ic)}$ ∈ $V_{N(dsc\text{-}ic)}$,

$S_{(dsc\text{-}ic)}$=DEBT_SERVICE1,

$P_{(dsc\text{-}ic)}$—set of productions:
  1. DEBT_SERVICE1 →HIGH_DEBTSERVICE1 I MEDIUM_DEBTSERVICE1 I LOW_DEBTSERVICE1
  2. **HIGH_DEBTSERVICE1** → CC
  3. **MEDIUM_DEBTSERVICE1** → BB I BC I CB
  4. **LOW_DEBTSERVICE1** → AA I AB I BA I AC I CA

    5. A → a
    6. B → b
    7. C → c.

Presented examples of cognitive information systems, supported management processes, are combinations of two different types of financial ratios.

The cognitive management systems allow to analyze the following cases:

- high debt service,
- medium debt service,
- low debt service.

In addition the cognitive analysis was conducted to merge the above selected subclasses of cognitive management systems. A cognitive analysis dedicated to cognitive financial management systems was proposed for particular classes:

In UBMLRSS-UBMPRSS systems were proposed the following subclasses:

- UBMLRSS-UBMPRSS-$G_{(mp\text{-}irr)}$ were analyzed the following ratios [15]:
  - v_{mp}—denotes the value of the mature payables ratio,
  - v_{irr}—denotes the value of the internal rate of return.

A sequential grammar being a grammatical formalism was defined for the above ratio describing the short-term liquidity and profitability of an enterprise. The linguistic formalism has the following form:

$$G_{(mp-irr)} = \left(V_{N(mp-irr)}, V_{T(mp-irr)}, P_{(mp-irr)}, S_{(mp-irr)} \right) \tag{6.15}$$

where

$V_{N(mp\text{-}irr)}$ = {LIQUIDITY_PROFITABILITY_MPIRR,
             EXCESS LIQUIDITY_STRONG PROFITABILITY_MPIRR,
             EXCESS LIQUIDITY_GOOD PROFITABILITY_ MPIRR,
             OPTIMAL LIQUIDITY_STRONG PROFITABILITY_MPIRR,
             OPTIMAL LIQUIDITY_GOOD PROFITABILITY_MPIRR,
             OPTIMAL LIQUIDITY_POOR PROFITABILITY_MPIRR,
             SOLVENCY PROBLEMS_POOR PROFITABILITY_ MPIRR,
             SOLVENCY PROBLEMS_UNPROFITABILITY_MPIRR}—the set of non-terminal
             symbols,
$V_{T(mp\text{-}irr)}$ = {a, b, c, d, e}, where
a ∈ [0; 1), b ∈ [1; 1,2], c ∈ (1,2; 2], d ∈ (2; + ∞), e ∈ [- 1; 0)—the set of terminal symbols,
$S_{(mp\text{-}irr)}$ ∈ $V_{N(mp\text{-}irr)}$,
$S_{(mp\text{-}irr)}$ = LIQUIDITY_PROFITABILITY_MPIRR,
$P_{(mp\text{-}irr)}$—set of productions:
    1. LIQUIDITY_PROFITABILITY_MPIRR →
        EXCESS LIQUIDITY_STRONG PROFITABILITY_MPIRR |
        EXCESS LIQUIDITY_GOOD PROFITABILITY_ MPIRR |
        OPTIMAL LIQUIDITY_STRONG PROFITABILITY_MPIRR |

      OPTIMAL LIQUIDITY_GOOD PROFITABILITY_MPIRR |
      OPTIMAL LIQUIDITY_POOR PROFITABILITY_MPIRR |
      SOLVENCY PROBLEMS_POOR PROFITABILITY_ MPIRR |
      SOLVENCY PROBLEMS_UNPROFITABILITY_MPIRR

2. **EXCESS LIQUIDITY_STRONG PROFITABILITY_MPIRR** → DC | DD
3. **EXCESS LIQUIDITY_GOOD PROFITABILITY_MPIRR** → DB
4. **OPTIMAL LIQUIDITY_STRONG PROFITABILITY_MPIRR** → BD | CD | BC | CC
5. **OPTIMAL LIQUIDITY_GOOD PROFITABILITY_MPIRR** → BB | CB
6. **OPTIMAL LIQUIDITY_POOR PROFITABILITY_MPIRR** → BA | CA | DA
7. **SOLVENCY PROBLEMS_POOR PROFITABILITY_MPIRR** → AA | AB| AC | AD
8. **SOLVENCY PROBLEMS_UNPROFITABILITY_MPIRR** → EA | EB | EC | ED | EE | AE | BE | CE | DE
9. A → a
10. B → b
11. C → c
12. D → d
13. E → e.

- UBMLRSS-UBMPRSS-$G_{(q\text{-}irr)}$ were analyzed the following ratios [15]:
  - v_q—denotes the value of the quick ratio,
  - v_{irr}—denotes the value of the internal rate of return.

The mathematical formalism has the following form:

$$G_{(q-irr)} = \left(V_{N(q-irr)}, V_{T(q-irr)}, P_{(q-irr)}, S_{(q-irr)}\right)$$ (6.16)

where

$V_{N(q\text{-}irr)}$ = {LIQUIDITY_PROFITABILITY_QIRR,
      EXCESS LIQUIDITY_STRONG PROFITABILITY_QIRR,
      EXCESS LIQUIDITY_GOOD PROFITABILITY_ QIRR,
      OPTIMAL LIQUIDITY_STRONG PROFITABILITY_QIRR,
      OPTIMAL LIQUIDITY_GOOD PROFITABILITY_QIRR,
      OPTIMAL LIQUIDITY_POOR PROFITABILITY_QIRR,
      SOLVENCY PROBLEMS_GOOD PROFITABILITY_ QIRR,
      SOLVENCY PROBLEMS_POOR PROFITABILITY_QIRR,
      SOLVENCY PROBLEMS_UNPROFITABILITY_QIRR}—the set of non-terminal
      symbols,
$V_{T(q\text{-}irr)}$ = {a, b, c, d, e}, where
a ∈ [0; 1), b ∈ [1; 1,2], c ∈ (1,2; 2], d ∈ (2; + ∞), e ∈ [-1; 0)—the set of terminal symbols,
$S_{(q\text{-}irr)}$ ∈ $V_{N(q\text{-}irr)}$,
$S_{(q\text{-}irr)}$ = LIQUIDITY_PROFITABILITY_QIRR,
$P_{(q\text{-}irr)}$—set of productions:
    1. LIQUIDITY_PROFITABILITY_QIRR →
      EXCESS LIQUIDITY_STRONG PROFITABILITY_QIRR |
      EXCESS LIQUIDITY_GOOD PROFITABILITY_ QIRR |
      OPTIMAL LIQUIDITY_STRONG PROFITABILITY_QIRR |

OPTIMAL LIQUIDITY_GOOD PROFITABILITY_QIRR |
OPTIMAL LIQUIDITY_POOR PROFITABILITY_QIRR |
SOLVENCY PROBLEMS_GOOD PROFITABILITY_ QIRR |
SOLVENCY PROBLEMS_POOR PROFITABILITY_QIRR |
SOLVENCY PROBLEMS_UNPROFITABILITY_QIRR

   2. **EXCESS LIQUIDITY_STRONG PROFITABILITY_QIRR** → DC | DD
   3. **EXCESS LIQUIDITY_GOOD PROFITABILITY_QIRR** → DB
   4. **OPTIMAL LIQUIDITY_STRONG PROFITABILITY_QIRR** → BD | CD | BC | CC
   5. **OPTIMAL LIQUIDITY_GOOD PROFITABILITY_QIRR** → BB | CB
   6. **OPTIMAL LIQUIDITY_POOR PROFITABILITY_QIRR** → BA | CA | DA
   7. **SOLVENCY PROBLEMS_GOOD PROFITABILITY_QIRR** → AB | AC | AD
   8. **SOLVENCY PROBLEMS_POOR PROFITABILITY_QIRR** → AA
   9. **SOLVENCY PROBLEMS_UNPROFITABILITY_QIRR** → EA | EB | EC | ED | EE |
      AE | BE | CE | DE
   10. A → a
   11. B → b
   12. C → c
   13. D → d
   14. E → e.

- UBMLRSS-UBMPRSS-$G_{(mp-q-irr)}$ were analyzed the following ratios [15]:
  - v_{mp}—denotes the value of the mature payables ratio,
  - v_q—denotes the value of the quick ratio,
  - v_{irr}—denotes the value of the internal rate of return.

The linguistic formalism has the following form:

$$G_{(mp-q-irr)} = \left(V_{N(mp-q-irr)}, V_{T(mp-q-irr)}, P_{(mp-q-irr)}, S_{(mp-q-irr)}\right) \tag{6.17}$$

where

$V_{N(mp-q-irr)}$ = {LIQUIDITY_PROFITABILITY_MPQIRR,
       EXCESS LIQUIDITY_STRONG PROFITABILITY_MPQIRR,
       EXCESS LIQUIDITY_GOOD PROFITABILITY_ MPQIRR,
       OPTIMAL LIQUIDITY_STRONG PROFITABILITY_ MPQIRR,
       OPTIMAL LIQUIDITY_GOOD PROFITABILITY_MPQIRR,
       OPTIMAL LIQUIDITY_POOR PROFITABILITY_MPQIRR,
       SOLVENCY PROBLEMS_POOR PROFITABILITY_MPQIRR,
       SOLVENCY PROBLEMS_ UNPROFITABILITY_MPQIRR}—the set of non-
       terminal symbols,
$V_{T(mp-q-irr)}$ = {a, b, c, d}, where
$a \in [0; 1)$, $b \in [1; 2]$, $c \in (2; +\infty)$, $d \in [-1; 0)$—the set of terminal symbols,
$S_{(mp-q-irr)} \in V_{N(mp-q-irr)}$,
$S_{(mp-q-irr)}$=LIQUIDITY_PROFITABILITY_MPQIRR,
$P_{(mp-q-irr)}$—set of productions:
   1. LIQUIDITY_PROFITABILITY_MPQIRR →

EXCESS LIQUIDITY_STRONG PROFITABILITY_MPQIRR |
EXCESS LIQUIDITY_GOOD PROFITABILITY_ MPQIRR |
OPTIMAL LIQUIDITY_STRONG PROFITABILITY_MPQIRR |
OPTIMAL LIQUIDITY_GOOD PROFITABILITY_MPQIRR |
OPTIMAL LIQUIDITY_POOR PROFITABILITY_MPQIRR |
SOLVENCY PROBLEMS_POOR PROFITABILITY_ MPQIRR |
SOLVENCY PROBLEMS_UNPROFITABILITY_MPQIRR

2. **EXCESS LIQUIDITY_STRONG PROFITABILITY_MPQIRR** → CCC
3. **EXCESS LIQUIDITY_GOOD PROFITABILITY_MPQIRR** → CCB | CBC | BCC
4. **OPTIMAL LIQUIDITY_STRONG PROFITABILITY_MPQIRR** → BBC | BCB | CBB
5. **OPTIMAL LIQUIDITY_GOOD PROFITABILITY_MPQIRR** → BBB | BAB | BAC | ABC | CAB | BCA | ACB | CBA | ABB
6. **OPTIMAL LIQUIDITY_POOR PROFITABILITY_MPQIRR** → BBA | ACC | CAC | CCA
7. **SOLVENCY PROBLEMS_POOR PROFITABILITY_MPQIRR** → AAA | ABA | ACA | BAA | CAA | AAB | AAC
8. **SOLVENCY PROBLEMS_UNPROFITABILITY_MPQIRR** → AAD | ABD | ACD | ADD | ADA | BAD | BBD | BCD | BDD | CAD | CBD | CCD | CDD | DAD | DBD | DCD | DDD | ADB | ADC | BDA | BDB | BDC | CDA | CDB | CDC | DAA | DAB | DAC | DBA | DBB | DBC | DCA | DCB | DCC | DDA | DDB | DDC
9. A → a
10. B → b
11. C → c
12. D → d.

- UBMLRSS-UBMPRSS-$G_{(cu-irr)}$ were analyzed the following ratios [15]:
  - v_{cu}—denotes the value of the current ratio,
  - v_{irr}—denotes the value of the internal rate of return.

The mathematical formalism has the following form:

$$G_{(cu-irr)} = \left(V_{N(cu-irr)}, V_{T(cu-irr)}, P_{(cu-irr)}, S_{(cu-irr)}\right)$$ (6.18)

where

$V_{N(cu-irr)}$ = {LIQUIDITY_PROFITABILITY_CUIRR,
EXCESS LIQUIDITY_STRONG PROFITABILITY_CUIRR,
EXCESS LIQUIDITY_GOOD PROFITABILITY_ CUIRR,
EXCESS LIQUIDITY_POOR PROFITABILITY_CUIRR,
OPTIMAL LIQUIDITY_STRONG PROFITABILITY_CUIRR,
OPTIMAL LIQUIDITY_GOOD PROFITABILITY_CUIRR,
SOLVENCY PROBLEMS_GOOD PROFITABILITY_ CUIRR,
SOLVENCY PROBLEMS_POOR PROFITABILITY_CUIRR,

SOLVENCY PROBLEMS_UNPROFITABILITY_CUIRR}—the set of non-terminal symbols,

$V_{T(cu-irr)}$ = {a, b, c, d, e}, where

a ∈ [0; 1), b ∈ [1; 1,2], c ∈ (1,2; 2], d ∈ (2; + ∞), e ∈ [-1; 0)—the set of terminal symbols,

$S_{(cu-irr)}$ ∈ $V_{N(cu-irr)}$,

$S_{(cu-irr)}$=LIQUIDITY_PROFITABILITY_CUIRR,

$P_{(cu-irr)}$—set of productions:

1. LIQUIDITY_PROFITABILITY_CUIRR →
   EXCESS LIQUIDITY_STRONG PROFITABILITY_CUIRR |
   EXCESS LIQUIDITY_GOOD PROFITABILITY_ CUIRR |
   EXCESS LIQUIDITY_POOR PROFITABILITY_CUIRR |
   OPTIMAL LIQUIDITY_STRONG PROFITABILITY_CUIRR |
   OPTIMAL LIQUIDITY_GOOD PROFITABILITY_CUIRR |
   SOLVENCY PROBLEMS_GOOD PROFITABILITY_ CUIRR |
   SOLVENCY PROBLEMS_POOR PROFITABILITY_CUIRR |
   SOLVENCY PROBLEMS_UNPROFITABILITY_CUIRR
2. **EXCESS LIQUIDITY_STRONG PROFITABILITY_CUIRR** → DC | DD
3. **EXCESS LIQUIDITY_GOOD PROFITABILITY_CUIRR** → DB
4. **EXCESS LIQUIDITY_POOR PROFITABILITY_CUIRR** → CA
5. **OPTIMAL LIQUIDITY_STRONG PROFITABILITY_CUIRR** → BD | CD | BC | CC
6. **OPTIMAL LIQUIDITY_GOOD PROFITABILITY_CUIRR** → BB | CB | BA | CA
7. **SOLVENCY PROBLEMS_GOOD PROFITABILITY_CUIRR** → AB | AC | AD
8. **SOLVENCY PROBLEMS_POOR PROFITABILITY_CUIRR** → AA
9. **SOLVENCY PROBLEMS_UNPROFITABILITY_CUIRR** → EA | EB | EC | ED | EE | AE | BE | CE | DE
10. A → a
11. B → b
12. C → c
13. D → d
14. E → e

- UBMLRSS-UBMPRSS-$G_{(cu-q-irr)}$ were analyzed the following ratios [15]:
  - v_{cu}—denotes the value of the current ratio,
  - v_q—denotes the value of the quick ratio,
  - v_{irr}—denotes the value of the internal rate of return.

The linguistic formalism has the following form:

$$G_{(cu-q-irr)} = \left(V_{N(cu-q-irr)}, V_{T(cu-q-irr)}, P_{(cu-q-irr)}, S_{(cu-q-irr)}\right)$$ (6.19)

where

$V_{N(cu-q-irr)}$ = {LIQUIDITY_PROFITABILITY_CUQIRR,
EXCESS LIQUIDITY_STRONG PROFITABILITY_CUQIRR,
EXCESS LIQUIDITY_GOOD PROFITABILITY_ CUQIRR,
EXCESS LIQUIDITY_POOR PROFITABILITY_CUQIRR,

OPTIMAL LIQUIDITY_STRONG PROFITABILITY_CUQIRR,
OPTIMAL LIQUIDITY_GOOD PROFITABILITY_CUQIRR,
OPTIMAL LIQUIDITY_POOR PROFITABILITY_CUQIRR,
SOLVENCY PROBLEMS_POOR PROFITABILITY_ CUQIRR,
SOLVENCY PROBLEMS_UNPROFITABILITY_CUQIRR}—the set of non-terminal symbols,

$V_{T(cu-q-irr)} = \{a, b, c, d\}$, where
$a \in [0; 1)$, $b \in [1; 2]$, $c \in (2; + \infty)$, $d \in [- 1; 0)$—the set of terminal symbols,
$S_{(cu-q-irr)} \in V_{N(cu-q-irr)}$,
$S_{(cu-q-irr)} = $ LIQUIDITY_PROFITABILITY_CUQIRR,
$P_{(cu-q-irr)}$—set of productions:

1. LIQUIDITY_PROFITABILITY_CUQIRR →
   EXCESS LIQUIDITY_STRONG PROFITABILITY_CUQIRR |
   EXCESS LIQUIDITY_GOOD PROFITABILITY_ CUQIRR |
   EXCESS LIQUIDITY_POOR PROFITABILITY_CUQIRR |
   OPTIMAL LIQUIDITY_STRONG PROFITABILITY_CUQIRR |
   OPTIMAL LIQUIDITY_GOOD PROFITABILITY_CUQIRR |
   OPTIMAL LIQUIDITY_POOR PROFITABILITY_ CUQIRR |
   SOLVENCY PROBLEMS_POOR PROFITABILITY_CUQIRR |
   SOLVENCY PROBLEMS_UNPROFITABILITY_CUQIRR
2. **EXCESS LIQUIDITY_STRONG PROFITABILITY_CUQIRR** → CCC
3. **EXCESS LIQUIDITY_GOOD PROFITABILITY_CUQIRR** → CCB | CBC | BCC
4. **EXCESS LIQUIDITY_POOR PROFITABILITY_CUQIRR** → CCA
5. **OPTIMAL LIQUIDITY_STRONG PROFITABILITY_CUQIRR** → BBC | BCB | CBB
6. **OPTIMAL LIQUIDITY_GOOD PROFITABILITY_CUQIRR** → BBB | BAB | BAC | ABC | CAB | BCA | ACB | CBA | ABB
7. **OPTIMAL LIQUIDITY_POOR PROFITABILITY_CUQIRR** → BBA | ACC | CAC
8. **SOLVENCY PROBLEMS_POOR PROFITABILITY_CUQIRR** → AAA | ABA | ACA | BAA | CAA | AAB | AAC
9. **SOLVENCY PROBLEMS_UNPROFITABILITY_CUQIRR** → AAD | ABD | ACD | ADD | ADA | BAD | BBD | BCD | BDD | CAD | CBD | CCD | CDD | DAD | DBD | DCD | DDD | ADB | ADC | BDA | BDB | BDC | CDA | CDB | CDC | DAA | DAB | DAC | DBA | DBB | DBC | DCA | DCB | DCC | DDA | DDB | DDC
10. A → a
11. B → b
12. C → c
13. D → d.

- UBMLRSS-UBMPRSS-$G_{(ca-irr)}$ were analyzed the following ratios [15]:
  - v_{ca}—denotes the value of the cash ratio,
  - v_{irr}—denotes the value of the internal rate of return.

The mathematical formalism for this example has the following form:

$$G_{(ca-irr)} = \left(V_{N(ca-irr)}, V_{T(ca-irr)}, P_{(ca-irr)}, S_{(ca-irr)}\right) \tag{6.20}$$

where

$V_{N(ca-irr)}$ = {LIQUIDITY_PROFITABILITY_CAIRR,
      EXCESS LIQUIDITY_STRONG PROFITABILITY_CAIRR,
      EXCESS LIQUIDITY_GOOD PROFITABILITY_ CAIRR,
      EXCESS LIQUIDITY_POOR PROFITABILITY_CAIRR,
      OPTIMAL LIQUIDITY_STRONG PROFITABILITY_CAIRR,
      OPTIMAL LIQUIDITY_GOOD PROFITABILITY_CAIRR,
      OPTIMAL LIQUIDITY_POOR PROFITABILITY_ CAIRR,
      SOLVENCY PROBLEMS_GOOD PROFITABILITY_CAIRR,
      SOLVENCY PROBLEMS_POOR PROFITABILITY_CAIRR,
      SOLVENCY PROBLEMS_ UNPROFITABILITY_CAIRR}—the set of non-terminal
      symbols,

$V_{T(ca-irr)}$ = {a, b, c, d, e}, where
$a \in [0; 1)$, $b \in [1; 1,2]$, $c \in (1,2; 2]$, $d \in (2; +\infty)$, $e \in [-1; 0)$—the set of terminal symbols,
$S_{(ca-irr)} \in V_{N(ca-irr)}$,
$S_{(ca-irr)}$=LIQUIDITY_PROFITABILITY_CAIRR,
$P_{(ca-irr)}$—set of productions:
    1. LIQUIDITY_PROFITABILITY_CAIRR →
    EXCESS LIQUIDITY_STRONG PROFITABILITY_CAIRR |
    EXCESS LIQUIDITY_GOOD PROFITABILITY_ CAIRR |
    EXCESS LIQUIDITY_POOR PROFITABILITY_CAIRR |
    OPTIMAL LIQUIDITY_STRONG PROFITABILITY_CAIRR |
    OPTIMAL LIQUIDITY_GOOD PROFITABILITY_CAIRR |
    OPTIMAL LIQUIDITY_POOR PROFITABILITY_ CAIRR |
    SOLVENCY PROBLEMS_GOOD PROFITABILITY_CAIRR |
    SOLVENCY PROBLEMS_POOR PROFITABILITY_CAIRR |
    SOLVENCY PROBLEMS_UNPROFITABILITY_CAIRR
    2. EXCESS LIQUIDITY_STRONG PROFITABILITY_CAIRR → DC I DD
    3. EXCESS LIQUIDITY_GOOD PROFITABILITY_CAIRR → DB
    4. EXCESS LIQUIDITY_POOR PROFITABILITY_CAIRR → DA
    5. OPTIMAL LIQUIDITY_STRONG PROFITABILITY_CAIRR → BD I CD I BC I CC
    6. OPTIMAL LIQUIDITY_GOOD PROFITABILITY_CAIRR → BB I CB
    7. OPTIMAL LIQUIDITY_POOR PROFITABILITY_CAIRR → BA I CA
    8. SOLVENCY PROBLEMS_GOOD PROFITABILITY_CAIRR → AB I AC I AD
    9. SOLVENCY PROBLEMS_POOR PROFITABILITY_CAIRR → AA
   10. SOLVENCY PROBLEMS_UNPROFITABILITY_CAIRR → EA I EB I EC I ED I EE I
    AE I BE I CE I DE
   11. A → a
   12. B → b
   13. C → c

14. D → d
15. E → e.

- UBMLRSS-UBMPRSS-$G_{(ca\text{-}q\text{-}irr)}$ were analyzed the following ratios [15]:
  - v_{ca}—denotes the value of the cash ratio,
  - v_q—denotes the value of the quick ratio,
  - v_{irr}—denotes the value of the internal rate of return.

The linguistic formalism for this example has the following form:

$$G_{(ca-q-irr)} = \left(V_{N(ca-q-irr)}, V_{T(ca-q-irr)}, P_{(ca-q-irr)}, S_{(ca-q-irr)}\right) \tag{6.21}$$

where

$V_{N(ca\text{-}q\text{-}irr)}$ = {LIQUIDITY_PROFITABILITY_CAQIRR,
EXCESS LIQUIDITY_STRONG PROFITABILITY_CAQIRR,
EXCESS LIQUIDITY_GOOD PROFITABILITY_ CAQIRR,
EXCESS LIQUIDITY_POOR PROFITABILITY_CAQIRR,
OPTIMAL LIQUIDITY_STRONG PROFITABILITY_CAQIRR,
OPTIMAL LIQUIDITY_GOOD PROFITABILITY_CAQIRR,
OPTIMAL LIQUIDITY_POOR PROFITABILITY_CAQIRR,
SOLVENCY PROBLEMS_GOOD PROFITABILITY_ CAQIRR,
SOLVENCY PROBLEMS_POOR PROFITABILITY_CAQIRR,
SOLVENCY PROBLEMS_UNPROFITABILITY_CAQIRR}—the set of non-terminal symbols,
$V_{T(ca\text{-}q\text{-}irr)}$ = {a, b, c, d}, where
a ∈ [0; 1), b ∈ [1; 2], c ∈ (2; + ∞), d ∈ [- 1; 0)—the set of terminal symbols,
$S_{(ca\text{-}q\text{-}irr)}$ ∈ $V_{N(ca\text{-}q\text{-}irr)}$,
$S_{(ca\text{-}q\text{-}irr)}$=LIQUIDITY_PROFITABILITY_CAQIRR,
$P_{(ca\text{-}q\text{-}irr)}$—set of productions:
  1. LIQUIDITY_PROFITABILITY_CAQIRR →
  EXCESS LIQUIDITY_STRONG PROFITABILITY_CAQIRR |
  EXCESS LIQUIDITY_GOOD PROFITABILITY_ CAQIRR |
  EXCESS LIQUIDITY_POOR PROFITABILITY_CAQIRR |
  OPTIMAL LIQUIDITY_STRONG PROFITABILITY_CAQIRR |
  OPTIMAL LIQUIDITY_GOOD PROFITABILITY_CAQIRR |
  OPTIMAL LIQUIDITY_POOR PROFITABILITY_ CAQIRR |
  SOLVENCY PROBLEMS_GOOD PROFITABILITY_CAQIRR |
  SOLVENCY PROBLEMS_POOR PROFITABILITY_CAQIRR |
  SOLVENCY PROBLEMS_UNPROFITABILITY_CAQIRR
  2. EXCESS LIQUIDITY_STRONG PROFITABILITY_CAQIRR → CCC
  3. EXCESS LIQUIDITY_GOOD PROFITABILITY_CAQIRR → CCB | CBC | BCC
  4. EXCESS LIQUIDITY_POOR PROFITABILITY_CAQIRR → CCA

5. **OPTIMAL LIQUIDITY_STRONG PROFITABILITY_CAQIRR** → BBC I BCB I CBB
6. **OPTIMAL LIQUIDITY_GOOD PROFITABILITY_CAQIRR** → BBB I BAB I BAC I ABC I CAB I BCA I ACB I CBA I ABB
7. **OPTIMAL LIQUIDITY_POOR PROFITABILITY_CAQIRR** → BBA I ACC I CAC
8. **SOLVENCY PROBLEMS_GOOD PROFITABILITY_CAQIRR** → AAB I AAC
9. **SOLVENCY PROBLEMS_POOR PROFITABILITY_CAQIRR** → AAA I ABA I ACA I BAA I CAA
10. **SOLVENCY PROBLEMS_UNPROFITABILITY_CAQIRR** → AAD I ABD I ACD I ADD I ADA I BAD I BBD I BCD I BDD I CAD I CBD I CCD I CDD I DAD I DBD I DCD I DDD I ADB I ADC I BDA I BDB I BDC I CDA I CDB I CDC I DAA I DAB I DAC I DBA I DBB I DBC I DCA I DCB I DCC I DDA I DDB I DDC
11. A → a
12. B → b
13. C → c
14. D → d.

Presented examples of cognitive information systems, supported management processes, are combinations of two or three different types of financial liquidity ratios, profitability ratios, and asset turnover indicators.

The cognitive management systems allow to analyze the following cases:

- excess liquidity and strong/good/poor profitability,
- optimal liquidity and strong/good/poor profitability,
- solvency problems and good/poor profitability,
- solvency problems and unprofitability.

In UBMARSS-UBMPRSS systems were proposed the following subclasses:

- UBMARSS-UBMPRSS-$G_{(ta-irr)}$ were analyzed the following ratios [15]:
    - v_{ta}—denotes the value of the total asset turnover indicator,
    - v_{irr}—denotes the value of the internal rate of return.

A sequential grammar formalism for this example has the following form:

$$G_{(ta-irr)} = \left(V_{N(ta-irr)}, V_{T(ta-irr)}, P_{(ta-irr)}, S_{(ta-irr)} \right) \tag{6.22}$$

where

$V_{N(ta\text{-}irr)}$ = {ASSET TURNOVER_PROFITABILITY_TAIRR,
HIGH TURNOVER_STRONG PROFITABILITY_TAIRR,
HIGH TURNOVER_GOOD PROFITABILITY_ TAIRR,
MEDIUM TURNOVER_STRONG PROFITABILITY_TAIRR,
MEDIUM TURNOVER_GOOD PROFITABILITY_TAIRR,
MEDIUM TURNOVER_POOR PROFITABILITY_TAIRR,
LOW TURNOVER_POOR PROFITABILITY_TAIRR,

LOW TURNOVER_UNPROFITABILITY_TAIRR}—the set of non-terminal
symbols,

$V_{T(ta\text{-}irr)}$ = {a, b, c, d, e}, where

a ∈ [0; 1), b ∈ [1; 2], c ∈ (2; 3], d ∈ (3; + ∞), e ∈ [- 1; 0)—the set of terminal symbols,

$S_{(ta\text{-}irr)}$ ∈ $V_{N(ta\text{-}irr)}$,

$S_{(ta\text{-}irr)}$=ASSET TURNOVER_PROFITABILITY_TAIRR,

$P_{(ta\text{-}irr)}$—set of productions:

1. ASSET TURNOVER_PROFITABILITY_TAIRR →
   HIGH TURNOVER_STRONG PROFITABILITY_TAIRR |
   HIGH TURNOVER_GOOD PROFITABILITY_TAIRR |
   MEDIUM TURNOVER_STRONG PROFITABILITY_TAIRR |
   MEDIUM TURNOVER_GOOD PROFITABILITY_TAIRR |
   MEDIUM TURNOVER_POOR PROFITABILITY_TAIRR |
   LOW TURNOVER_POOR PROFITABILITY_TAIRR |
   LOW TURNOVER_UNPROFITABILITY_TAIRR
2. **HIGH TURNOVER_STRONG PROFITABILITY_TAIRR** → DC I DD
3. **HIGH TURNOVER_GOOD PROFITABILITY_TAIRR** → DA I DB
4. **MEDIUM TURNOVER_STRONG PROFITABILITY_TAIRR** → BC I BD I CC I CD
5. **MEDIUM TURNOVER_GOOD PROFITABILITY_TAIRR** → BB I CB I AC I AD
6. **MEDIUM TURNOVER_POOR PROFITABILITY_TAIRR** → BA I CA
7. **LOW TURNOVER_POOR PROFITABILITY_TAIRR** → AA I AB
8. **LOW TURNOVER_UNPROFITABILITY_CAIRR** → EA I EB I EC I ED I EE I AE |
   BE I CE I DE
9. A → a
10. B → b
11. C → c
12. D → d
13. E → e.

- UBMARSS-UBMPRSS-$G_{(wa\text{-}irr)}$ were analyzed the following ratios [15]:
  - v_{wa}—denotes the value of the working asset turnover indicator,
  - v_{irr}—denotes the value of the internal rate of return.

A sequential grammar being a grammatical formalism was defined for the above ratio describing the activity and profitability of an enterprise. The linguistic formalism has the following form:

$$G_{(wa-irr)} = \left(V_{N(wa-irr)}, V_{T(wa-irr)}, P_{(wa-irr)}, S_{(wa-irr)} \right)$$ (6.23)

where

$V_{N(wa\text{-}irr)}$ = {ASSET TURNOVER_PROFITABILITY_WAIRR,
        HIGH TURNOVER_STRONG PROFITABILITY_WAIRR,
        HIGH TURNOVER_GOOD PROFITABILITY_WAIRR,
        MEDIUM TURNOVER_STRONG PROFITABILITY_WAIRR,
        MEDIUM TURNOVER_GOOD PROFITABILITY_WAIRR,

MEDIUM TURNOVER_POOR PROFITABILITY_WAIRR,
LOW TURNOVER_GOOD PROFITABILITY_WAIRR,
LOW TURNOVER_POOR PROFITABILITY_WAIRR,
LOW TURNOVER_ UNPROFITABILITY_WAIRR}—the set of non-terminal symbols,

$V_{T(wa\text{-}irr)}$ = {a, b, c, d, e}, where
a ∈ [0; 1), b ∈ [1; 2], c ∈ (2; 3], d ∈ (3; + ∞), e ∈ [−1; 0)—the set of terminal symbols,

$S_{(wa\text{-}irr)}$ ∈ $V_{N(wa\text{-}irr)}$,

$S_{(wa\text{-}irr)}$=ASSET TURNOVER_PROFITABILITY_WAIRR,

$P_{(wa\text{-}irr)}$—set of productions:
1. ASSET TURNOVER_PROFITABILITY_WAIRR →
   HIGH TURNOVER_STRONG PROFITABILITY_WAIRR |
   HIGH TURNOVER_GOOD PROFITABILITY_WAIRR |
   MEDIUM TURNOVER_STRONG PROFITABILITY_WAIRR |
   MEDIUM TURNOVER_GOOD PROFITABILITY_WAIRR |
   MEDIUM TURNOVER_POOR PROFITABILITY_WAIRR |
   LOW TURNOVER_GOOD PROFITABILITY_ WAIRR |
   LOW TURNOVER_POOR PROFITABILITY_WAIRR |
   LOW TURNOVER_UNPROFITABILITY_WAIRR
2. **HIGH TURNOVER_STRONG PROFITABILITY_WAIRR** → DC | DD
3. **HIGH TURNOVER_GOOD PROFITABILITY_WAIRR** → DA | DB
4. **MEDIUM TURNOVER_STRONG PROFITABILITY_WAIRR** → BC | BD | CC | CD
5. **MEDIUM TURNOVER_GOOD PROFITABILITY_WAIRR** → BB | CB
6. **MEDIUM TURNOVER_POOR PROFITABILITY_WAIRR** → BA | CA
7. **LOW TURNOVER_GOOD PROFITABILITY_WAIRR** → AB | AC | AD
8. **LOW TURNOVER_POOR PROFITABILITY_WAIRR** → AA
9. **LOW TURNOVER_UNPROFITABILITY_WAIRR** → EA | EB | EC | ED | EE | AE | BE | CE | DE
10. A → a
11. B → b
12. C → c
13. D → d
14. E → e.

- UBMARSS-UBMPRSS-$G_{(ta\text{-}wa\text{-}irr)}$ were analyzed the following ratios [15]:
  - v_{ta}—denotes the value of the total asset turnover indicator,
  - v_{wa}—denotes the value of the working asset turnover indicator,
  - v_{irr}—denotes the value of the internal rate of return.

A sequential grammar formalism for this example has the following form:

$$G_{(ta-wa-irr)} = \left(V_{N(ta-wa-irr)}, V_{T(ta-wa-irr)}, P_{(ta-wa-irr)}, S_{(ta-wa-irr)} \right) \qquad (6.24)$$

where

$V_{N(ta\text{-}wa\text{-}irr)}$ = {ASSET TURNOVER_PROFITABILITY_TAWAIRR,

HIGH TURNOVER_ STRONG PROFITABILITY_TAWAIRR,
HIGH TURNOVER_GOOD PROFITABILITY_TAWAIRR,
MEDIUM TURNOVER_STRONG PROFITABILITY_TAWAIRR,
MEDIUM TURNOVER_GOOD PROFITABILITY_ TAWAIRR,
MEDIUM TURNOVER_POOR PROFITABILITY_TAWAIRR,
LOW TURNOVER_GOOD PROFITABILITY_TAWAIRR,
LOW TURNOVER_POOR PROFITABILITY_TAWAIRR,
LOW TURNOVER_UNPROFITABILITY_ TAWAIRR}—the set of non-terminal symbols,

$V_{T(ta\text{-}wa\text{-}irr)} = \{a, b, c, d\}$, where
$a \in [0; 1)$, $b \in [1; 3]$, $c \in (3; +\infty)$, $d \in [-1; 0)$—the set of terminal symbols,
$S_{(ta\text{-}wa\text{-}irr)} \in V_{N(ta\text{-}wa\text{-}irr)}$,
$S_{(ta\text{-}wa\text{-}irr)}$=ASSET TURNOVER_PROFITABILITY_TAWAIRR,
$P_{(ta\text{-}wa\text{-}irr)}$—set of productions:

1. ASSET TURNOVER_PROFITABILITY_TAWAIRR →
   HIGH TURNOVER_STRONG PROFITABILITY_TAWAIRR |
   HIGH TURNOVER_GOOD PROFITABILITY_ TAWAIRR |
   MEDIUM TURNOVER_STRONG PROFITABILITY_TAWAIRR |
   MEDIUM TURNOVER_GOOD PROFITABILITY_TAWAIRR |
   MEDIUM TURNOVER_POOR PROFITABILITY_TAWAIRR |
   LOW TURNOVER_GOOD PROFITABILITY_TAWAIRR |
   LOW TURNOVER_POOR PROFITABILITY_ TAWAIRR |
   LOW TURNOVER_UNPROFITABILITY_TAWAIRR
2. **HIGH TURNOVER_STRONG PROFITABILITY_TAWAIRR** → CCC | BCC | CBC
3. **HIGH TURNOVER_GOOD PROFITABILITY_TAWAIRR** → CCA | CCB | CBB
4. **MEDIUM TURNOVER_STRONG PROFITABILITY_TAWAIRR** → BBC | ACC | BAC | BCB | CAC
5. **MEDIUM TURNOVER_GOOD PROFITABILITY_TAWAIRR** → BBB | ABB | ABC | ACB | BAB | CAB
6. **MEDIUM TURNOVER_POOR PROFITABILITY_TAWAIRR** → BBA | ACA | BAA | BCA | CAA | CBA
7. **LOW TURNOVER_GOOD PROFITABILITY_TAWAIRR** → AAB | AAC
8. **LOW TURNOVER_POOR PROFITABILITY_TAWAIRR** → AAA | ABA
9. **LOW TURNOVER_UNPROFITABILITY_TAWAIRR** → AAD | ABD | ACD | ADD | BAD | BBD | BCD | BDD | CAD | CBD | CCD | CDD | DAD | DBD | DCD | DDD | ADA | ADB | ADC | BDA | BDB | BDC | CDA | CDB | CDC | DAA | DAB | DAC | DBA | DBB | DBC | DCA | DCB | DCC | DDA | DDB | DDC
10. A → a
11. B → b
12. C → c
13. D → d.

Presented examples of cognitive information systems, supported management processes, are combinations of two or three different types of financial ratios.

The cognitive management systems allow to analyze the following cases:

- high turnover and strong/good profitability,
- medium turnover and strong/good/poor profitability,
- low turnover and good/poor profitability,
- low turnover and unprofitability.

Examples of cognitive systems for the semantic analysis of data dedicated to supporting processes of managing data/information show how these processes can be improved and in what area they can be applied. The presented examples of cognitive management systems related to analyses of selected types of data—financial ratios—whose analysis is based on interpreting the current standing and projecting the future one. The determinants of the described standing are recognized by the system as one of a whole group of factors, which influence the future condition of the analyzed entity.

The main idea of cognitive management systems was to improve the management processes of datasets. The cognitive management systems supporting the management processes by [3]:

- analysis of the internal/external situation of the company,
- predicting the future situation,
- improving decision-making processes,
- supporting strategic decisions,
- supporting enterprise management processes in the local and global aspects.

The main measure for assessing cognitive systems supporting management processes and dedicated to analyzing information contained in sets of financial ratios is the effectiveness of the proposed solutions.

The comparison of cognitive information systems supporting management processes by semantic analysis of financial ratios presents Table 6.1.

6.5 EXAMPLES OF APPLICATION DOMAINS AND FUTURE PERSPECTIVES

Areas in which cognitive systems can be used are extremely diverse. They range from image analysis, through the identification analysis performed using personal identification, biometric identification and marking, all the way to systems supporting management processes. This last class of semantic interpretation systems—cognitive management systems—is used to support various processes taking place in enterprises, organizations, etc.

The essence of the solutions discussed is a process based on the semantic analysis of the interpreted sets of data/information. Extracting layers of semantics, analyzing and interpreting them the analyzed data to be understood more fully. The understanding process ranks the determinants of a given condition. The more important they are, the greater their significance for "creating" information, data, situations, etc.

Table 6.1 The Comparison of Cognitive Information Systems Supporting Management Processes by Semantic Analysis of Selected Financial Ratios

Class of Cognitive Systems	Subclass of Cognitive Systems	Simple Class of Cognitive Systems	Combined Class of Cognitive Systems	Kind of Analyzed Financial Ratios				Number of Analyzed Ratios	Name of Analyzed Ratio
				Turnover Ratio	Financial Leverage Ratio	Profitability Ratio	Liquidity Ratio		
UBMLRSS	UBMLRSS-$G_{(cu-q)}$	x	–	–	–	–	x	2	The current ratio The quick ratio
	UBMLRSS-$G_{(cu-q-ca)}$	x	–	–	–	–	x	3	The current ratio The quick ratio The cash ratio
	UBMLRSS-$G_{(cu-q-mp)}$	x	–	–	–	–	x	3	The current ratio The quick ratio The mature payables ratio
	UBMLRSS-$G_{(cu-ca-mp)}$	x	–	–	–	–	x	3	The current ratio The cash ratio The mature payables ratio
	UBMLRSS-$G_{(q-ca-mp)}$	x	–	–	–	–	x	3	The quick ratio The cash ratio The mature payables ratio
	UBMLRSS-$G_{(cu-q-ca-tr)}$	x	–	–	–	–	x	4	The current ratio The quick ratio The cash ratio The treasury ratio
UBMARSS	UBMARSS-$G_{(ta-la)}$	x	–	x	–	–	–	2	The total asset turnover The liquid asset turnover
	UBMARSS-$G_{(ta-wa)}$	x	–	x	–	–	–	2	The total asset turnover The working asset turnover
	UBMARSS-$G_{(ta-wa-la)}$	x	–	x	–	–	–	3	The total asset turnover The working asset turnover The liquid asset turnover
UBMPRSS	UBMPRSS-$G_{(rna-rga-rgi)}$	x	–	–	–	x	–	3	The return on net assets The return on gross assets The return on gross assets including interest
	UBMPRSS-$G_{(rfa-rwa-rca)}$	x	–	–	–	x	–	3	The return on fixed assets The return on working assets The return on clear assets

(*Continued*)

Table 6.1 The Comparison of Cognitive Information Systems Supporting Management Processes by Semantic Analysis of Selected Financial Ratios (Continued)

Class of Cognitive Systems	Subclass of Cognitive Systems	Simple Class of Cognitive Systems	Combined Class of Cognitive Systems	Kind of Analyzed Financial Ratios				Number of Analyzed Ratios	Name of Analyzed Ratio
				Turnover Ratio	Financial Leverage Ratio	Profitability Ratio	Liquidity Ratio		
UBMFLRSS	UBMFLRSS-$G_{(td-ld)}$	x	–	–	x	–	–	2	The total debt ratio / The long-term debt ratio
	UBMFLRSS-$G_{(td-ls)}$	x	–	–	x	–	–	2	The total debt ratio / The liability structure ratio
	UBMFLRSS-$G_{(dsc-ic)}$	x	–	–	x	–	–	2	The debt service coverage ratio / The interest coverage ratio
UBMLRSS-UBMPRSS	UBMLRSS-UBMPRSS-$G_{(mp-irr)}$	–	x	–	–	x	x	2	The mature payables ratio / The internal rate of return
	UBMLRSS-UBMPRSS-$G_{(q-irr)}$	–	x	–	–	x	x	2	The quick ratio / The internal rate of return
	UBMLRSS-UBMPRSS-$G_{(mp-q-irr)}$	–	x	–	–	x	x	3	The mature payables ratio / The quick ratio / The internal rate of return
	UBMLRSS-UBMPRSS-$G_{(cu-irr)}$	–	x	–	–	x	x	2	The current ratio / The internal rate of return
	UBMLRSS-UBMPRSS-$G_{(cu-q-irr)}$	–	x	–	–	x	x	3	The current ratio / The quick ratio / The internal rate of return
	UBMLRSS-UBMPRSS-$G_{(ca-irr)}$	–	x	–	–	x	x	2	The cash ratio / The internal rate of return
	UBMLRSS-UBMPRSS-$G_{(ca-q-irr)}$	–	x	–	–	x	x	3	The cash ratio / The quick ratio / The internal rate of return
UBMARSS-UBMPRSS	UBMARSS-UBMPRSS-$G_{(ta-irr)}$	–	x	x	–	x	–	2	The total asset turnover / The internal rate of return
	UBMARSS-UBMPRSS-$G_{(wa-irr)}$	–	x	x	–	x	–	2	The working asset turnover / The internal rate of return
	UBMARSS-UBMPRSS-$G_{(ta-wa-irr)}$	–	x	x	–	x	–	3	The total asset turnover / The working asset turnover / The internal rate of return

Today, the development directions of cognitive management systems are suggesting the directions in which this discipline will develop, such as strategic management, information/data management, management in the areas of business operations, managing individual sectors of public life, etc. [20–22].

Cognitive management systems will be used to support management processes in areas in which a semantic analysis can be carried out.

REFERENCES

[1] Ogiela L: Data management in cognitive financial systems. *Int J Inf Manage* 33:263–270, 2013.

[2] Ogiela L: Towards cognitive economy. *Soft Comput* 18(9):1675–1683, 2014.

[3] Ogiela L, Ogiela MR: Computer-aided knowledge extraction and management for decision supporting processes. In: *ICNS 2015—the eleventh International Conference on Networking and Services (ICNS 2015), May 24–29, 2015, Rome, Italy, IARIA, 2015*, pp 86–91.

[4] Bernstein L, Wild J: Analysis of financial statements, ed 5, 1999, Amazon.

[5] Cohen H, Lefebvre C, editors: Handbook of categorization in cognitive science, The Netherlands, 2005, Elsevier.

[6] Ogiela L, Ogiela MR: Cognitive management systems. In: *IMIS 2014—the eighth international conference on Innovative Mobile and Internet Services in ubiquitous computing (IMIS-2014), 2–4 July 2014, Birmingham City University, Birmingham, UK*, pp 192–195.

[7] Buchanan S, McMenemy D: Digital service analysis and design: the role of process modelling. *Int J Inf Manage* 32(3):251–256, 2012.

[8] Ogiela L, Ogiela MR: Semantic analysis processes in advanced pattern understanding systems. In: Kim T-H, et al., editors: *Advanced computer science and information technology, communications in computer and information science*, vol. 195, Berlin Heidelberg, 2011, Springer-Verlag, pp 26–30.

[9] Zhong N, Raś ZW, Tsumoto S, Suzuki E, editors: *Foundations of intelligent systems, 14th international symposium, ISMIS, Maebashi City, Japan*, 2003.

[10] Ogiela L: Advanced techniques for knowledge management and access to strategic information. *Int J Inf Manage* 35:154–159, 2015.

[11] Ogiela L, Ogiela MR: Semantic data analysis algorithms supporting decision-making processes. In: Barolli L et al., editors: *10th International conference on broadband and wireless computing, communication and applications, Krakow, Poland, 4–6 November 2015*, pp. 494–496.

[12] Ogiela MR, Ogiela L, Ogiela U: Security and privacy in distributed information management. In: *2014 International conference on Intelligent Networking and Collaborative Systems (IEEE INCoS 2014), Salerno, Italy, September 10–12, 2014*, pp 73–78.

[13] Laudon KC, Laudon JP: Management information systems—managing the digital firm, ed 7, Upper Saddle River, NJ, 2002, Prentice-Hall International Inc.

[14] Ogiela L: Intelligent techniques for secure financial management in cloud computing. *Electron Commer Res Appl* 14:456–464, 2015.

[15] Ogiela L, Ogiela MR: Comparison of cognitive information systems supporting management tasks. In: *The 7th international conference on Intelligent Networking and Collaborative Systems (INCoS-2015), September 2–4 2015, Taipei, Taiwan*, pp 49–56.

[16] Ogiela L, Ogiela MR: Efficiency of cognitive information systems supporting enterprise management tasks. In: *9th International conference on Innovative Mobile and Internet Services in ubiquitous computing (IMIS-2015), Blumenau, Santa Catarina, Brazil, 08–10 July 2015*, pp 166–170.

[17] Ogiela L, Ogiela MR: Computer-aided enterprise management. In: Xhafa F, et al., editors: *Ninth international conference on P2P, Parallel, Grid, Cloud and Internet Computing (3PGCIC), Guangzhou, People R China, November 08–10, 2014*, pp 282–285.

[18] Ogiela L, Ogiela MR: Management information systems. In: Park JJH, et al., editors: *Ubiquitous Computing Application and Wireless Sensor, UCAWSN-2014, Lecture notes in electrical engineering*, vol. 331, Dordrecht Heidelberg New York London, 2015, Springer, pp 449–456.

[19] Ogiela MR, Ogiela L, Ogiela U: Cryptographic techniques in advanced information management. In: *IMIS 2014—The eighth international conference on Innovative Mobile and Internet Services in ubiquitous computing (IMIS-2014), 2–4 July 2014, Birmingham, UK*, pp 254–257.

[20] Branquinho J, editor: The foundations of cognitive science, Oxford, 2001, Clarendon Press.

[21] Ekman P: Facial expressions and emotion. *Am Psychol* 48:348–392, 1993.

[22] TalebiFard P, Leung VCM: Context-aware mobility management in heterogeneous network environments. *J Wireless Mobile Networks, Ubiquitous Comput Dependable Appl* 2(2):19–32, 2011.

SUMMARY

Cognitive information systems have become the main thread of this book. Their development by the author of this book has made it necessary to describe the results of the research work carried out over many years. The solutions produced are now presented to the readers to show them the various directions in which semantic data analysis can be used and the breadth of the opportunities for their future application [1–5]. When summarizing the whole book, it is worth emphasizing that every chapter of it is a study of a subject connected with cognitive information systems, focusing the topic of the book on cognitive management systems.

Chapter 1, Introduction, presents aspects connected with cognitive science that introduce the reader to the arcana of cognitive topics [5,6]. The aspects of the historical development of concepts associated with cognitive science are discussed and their significance for the development of related disciplines is identified. Human cognitive processes taking place in the human mind are adopted as the basis of the operation of cognitive solutions. The relations between the analysis and interpretation processes characteristic for humans and their computer imitations are discussed. Disciplines making up cognitive science are presented by reference to cognitive subjects.

Chapter 2, The Fundamentals of Cognitive Informatics, characterizes subjects connected with the development of cognitive informatics and processes influencing the creation of this new branch of informatics [2,7]. Cognitive informatics was created by combining various scientific disciplines in which an important role is played by processes by which the human brain operates. These processes, transferred to the area of systems solutions, formed the foundation for the cognitive topics. Introducing a definition of cognitive science and determining the relations between the different disciplines within it offer the opportunity to apply the developed solutions in various types of analyses. Particular importance should be assigned to the ability to adapt semantic data analysis techniques to describing and interpreting complex sets of information. This process, executed in semantic data analysis systems, supports the semantic interpretation and reasoning based on the analyzed sets of information.

Chapter 3, Intelligent Computer Data Analysis Techniques, discusses techniques of intelligent data analysis [8,9]. The concept of an in-depth data analysis is introduced, which is understood as the semantic analysis of data. The ability to extract the meaning from sets of analyzed data means that analysis processes are supplemented with the ability to interpret the sets of data/information undergoing the analysis. Semantic analysis can be performed using linguistic methods in the process of describing and interpreting datasets. Cognitive information systems portray the course and the execution of the complex process of analyzing and interpreting data. This process applies both to the tasks of classifying and recognizing the analyzed data, as well as to the processes of understanding the analyzed sets.

Cognitive Information Systems in Management Sciences. DOI: http://dx.doi.org/10.1016/B978-0-12-803803-1.00007-0

Chapter 4, The Fundamentals of Management Sciences, presents primary aspects of management processes [10–12]. These processes concern both simple tasks of supporting decision-making, but also improving decision-making by the semantic interpretation of situations and events that are analyzed. Their reference point consists, therefore, in processes of managing knowledge and information. The correct execution of these processes implies the need to introduce stages at which the meaning contained in datasets will be understood. A management process supplemented with the semantic interpretation of the analyzed information sets forms an example of a complex decision-making process dedicated to supporting processes of data management.

Chapter 5, Cognitive Information Systems, presents a new generation of systems referred to as cognitive systems [2,3]. The feature that distinguishes this class of systems from other information systems is semantic data analysis. This solution is founded on assessing the impact of the analyzed datasets on phenomena, situations, states, etc. Cognitive information systems have been defined and discussed based on a characterization of perception models associated with information analysis processes. In addition a classification of cognitive systems was introduced and the methods of taking decisions in cognitive information systems were discussed. A special role has been assigned to the process of taking decisions in cognitive systems. This process has been supplemented with the semantic analysis of the interpreted information/data, which constitute the most important element in the operation of cognitive data analysis systems.

Chapter 6, Intelligent Cognitive Information Systems in Management Applications discusses information systems for the semantic analysis of data, dedicated to supporting the process of managing information [3,13]. Cognitive systems for the semantic analysis of data are aimed at supporting and improving data management processes. Management processes can be supported by using linguistic techniques for the semantic interpretation of the analyzed sets of information/data, performed at the description and interpretation stage. Semantic interpretation techniques allow information that significantly describes the meaning of the data for the entire analysis process to be extracted from the sets of analyzed data. Understanding these aspects makes it possible to improve the entire process of taking decisions, particularly strategic ones.

REFERENCES

[1] Laudon KC, Laudon JP: Management information systems—managing the digital firm, ed 7, Upper Saddle River, NJ, 2002, Prentice-Hall International Inc.
[2] Ogiela L, Ogiela MR: Cognitive management systems. In: *IMIS 2014—the eighth international conference on Innovative Mobile and Internet Services in ubiquitous computing (IMIS-2014), 2–4 July 2014, Birmingham City University, Birmingham, UK*, pp 192–195.
[3] Ogiela L, Ogiela MR: Management information systems. In: Park JJH et al., editors: *Ubiquitous Computing Application and Wireless Sensor, UCAWSN-2014, Lecture notes in electrical engineering*, vol. 331, Dordrecht Heidelberg New York London, 2015, Springer, pp 449–456.
[4] Zhong N, Raś ZW, Tsumoto S, Suzuki E, editors: *Foundations of intelligent systems*, 14th international symposium, Maebashi City, Japan, 2003, ISMIS.
[5] Branquinho J, editor: The foundations of cognitive science, Oxford, 2001, Clarendon Press.
[6] Ogiela L: Towards cognitive economy. *Soft Comput* 18(9):1675–1683, 2014.

[7] Ogiela L, Ogiela MR: Comparison of cognitive information systems supporting management tasks. In: *The 7th international conference on Intelligent Networking and Collaborative Systems (INCoS-2015), September 2–4, 2015, Taipei, Taiwan*, pp 49–56.

[8] Ogiela L, Ogiela MR: Computer-aided enterprise management. In: Xhafa F, et al., editors: *Ninth international conference on P2P, Parallel, Grid, Cloud and Internet Computing (3PGCIC), Guangzhou, People R China, November 08–10, 2014*, pp 282–285.

[9] Ogiela L, Ogiela MR: Semantic data analysis algorithms supporting decision-making processes. In: Barolli L, et al., editors: *10th International conference on broadband and wireless computing, communication and applications, Krakow, Poland, 4–6 November 2015*, pp 494–496.

[10] Ogiela L: Data management in cognitive financial systems. *Int J Inf Manage* 33:263–270, 2013.

[11] Ogiela L, Ogiela MR: Computer-aided knowledge extraction and management for decision supporting processes. In: *ICNS 2015—the eleventh International Conference on Networking and Services (ICNS 2015), May 24–29, 2015, Rome, Italy*, IARIA, 2015, pp 86–91.

[12] Ogiela MR, Ogiela L, Ogiela U: Cryptographic techniques in advanced information management. In: *IMIS 2014—the eighth international conference on Innovative Mobile and Internet Services in Ubiquitous Computing (IMIS-2014), 2–4 July 2014, Birmingham, UK*, pp 254–257.

[13] Ogiela MR, Ogiela L, Ogiela U: Security and privacy in distributed information management. In: *2014 International conference on Intelligent Networking and Collaborative Systems (IEEE INCoS 2014), Salerno, Italy, September 10–12, 2014*, pp 73–78.

Index

H

Hierarchical web structure, 70
Human cognitive processes, 4, 64
Human data perception and analysis, 67
Human perception models in cognitive data analysis and
    decision-making, 64–67
  cognitive computer models, 66, 66*f*
  cognitive informatics model, 66
  cognitive information representation model, 65*f*
  model of information representation in human brain, 64–65
  models of cognitive machines, 67, 67*f*
  NeI (Neural informatics model), 66

I

Identification analysis processes, 20
Image recognition processes, 39
IMIS. *See* Integrated management information system (IMIS)
Information
  flow in cognitive management systems, 81–82, 83*f*,
    84*f*, 85*f*
  information retrieval process, memory features appearing
    during, 7*f*
  logistics systems, 52–53
  management, 79–80
    processes, 48, 51
    system security, 51
  representation model, 64–65
  systems, 25–26, 57
    analysis of, 25
    classification, 25
    description concepts, 27*f*
    disciplines, 26*f*
    security systems, 51
Integrated data management systems, 54*f*, 55
Integrated management information system (IMIS), 53
Intelligence levels, 29
Intelligent cognitive information systems
  application domains and future perspectives, 118
  information flow in, 81–82, 83*f*, 84*f*, 85*f*
  interpretation and data analysis processes in, 90–95, 94*f*
  in management applications, 79, 82–90, 86*f*
  use cases in management applications, 95–118, 119*t*–120*t*
Intelligent computer data analysis techniques, 25
  classification procedures, 39–41
    assigning unknown object, 39*f*, 40*f*
    classification of object recognition methods, 41*f*
    similarities between analyzed datasets and pattern, 39*f*
  computational intelligence description approaches, 41–42
  data
    processing, 32–36
    recognition, 36–38
    understanding, 36–38, 37*f*
  disciplines, 26*f*
  information interpretation stage, 30

information systems, 25–26
  analysis of, 25
  classification, 25
  description concepts, 27*f*
  disciplines, 26*f*
intelligent information systems, 26–27, 30
  components of, 31*f*
  operation of, 30
mathematical formalisms, 27–28
neuron, 31
process of data analysis, 38*f*
semantic analysis, 32
structural approach, 29
structural methods, 28
Intelligent information systems, 26–27, 79
Interpretation
  in cognitive management system, 90–95, 94*f*
  process, 74

K

Knowledge management systems, 47–48
  knowledge layers in, 47*f*

L

Learning processes, 4–7
  process of semantic analysis and data, 22*f*
Linguistic formalisms, 75, 80
Linguistic perception algorithm, 38
Linguistic reasoning algorithm, 16
Logistics information systems (LIS), 53, 55
L_{PDL} description languages, 35
L_{SFDL} description languages, 35

M

Management information systems (MIS), 55
Management processes, 45
  computational intelligence in data analysis, 52–58
    cognitive analysis aspects in management systems, 56*f*
    decision-making support in information systems, 57
    features of integrated management systems, 53
    integrated data management systems, 54*f*
    intelligent information systems, 52
    scope of management information systems, 55
    semantic layers of analyzed datasets, 58
Management sciences
  characteristic features, 45–46
  computational intelligence in data analysis in management
    processes, 52–58
  decision processes in, 52–58
  decision-makers, 46
  knowledge layers in knowledge management systems, 47*f*
  management theory, 45
  use of information management processes, 47–48

Printed in the United States
By Bookmasters